The 'F' Word

The 'F' Word

✦

Good Words for Great Leaders

David Paul Eich

iUniverse, Inc.
New York Bloomington Shanghai

The 'F' Word
Good Words for Great Leaders

iUniverse books may be ordered through booksellers or by contacting:

iUniverse
1663 Liberty Drive
Bloomington, IN 47403
www.iuniverse.com
1-800-Authors (1-800-288-4677)

ISBN: 978-0-595-48355-6 (pbk)
ISBN: 978-0-595-48761-5 (cloth)
ISBN: 978-0-595-60445-6 (ebk)

Printed in the United States of America

Contents

ACKNOWLEDGEMENTS

There are a number of people who helped me pull this work together. Robert Polk stepped forward to offer his outstanding editorial skills. Jill Oesterle saved me from myself as she prepared the manuscript for the publisher. Without their talents, I would have nothing but words on paper. Thank you.

My loving wife, Cindy, allowed her husband to tell the unbelievable story of how we met forty-four years ago. To Rob, Andrew, and Kelly, thank you for providing your dad with the material I needed to make a point or share a memory. To my family, I am forever grateful.

A special acknowledgement goes out to those individuals who were kind enough to let me tell their story. Though there are too many to mention, I do want to acknowledge one very special person whose leadership, passion, and faith have set the bar for so many people: John Shinsky. Thank you John, for building an orphanage for children, inviting others to share your dream, and trusting that God will never abandon you. You are an inspiration to all of us.

It is to you, John, and your lovely wife, Cindy, that I dedicate this book.

INTRODUCTION

QUO VADIS?

The English translation means, *"Where are you going?"* In a curious way this simple Latin phrase is what this book is all about. CEO's and other senior management, may point to their organization's strategic plan to help answer the question. Managers and supervisors may choose to focus on volume goals, departmental budgets, turnover rates, financial objectives, or some other metric commonly associated with the business world. Teachers might answer the question in terms of student pass/fail rates; coaches, win/loss records; pastors, congregation attendance; military officers, captured enemy combatants; judges, reduced caseloads; or politicians, the size of their campaign "war chest." And as for parents, these critical leaders may simply measure their success through the accomplishments of their children.

Many of today's books on leadership entice readers with headline titles such as, *First Break All the Rules, What Got You Here Won't Get You There,* and my favorite, *Run With the Bulls Without Getting Trampled.* Other authors prefer a numerical approach to include the following: *81 Challenges Smart Managers Face, 151 Quick Ideas to Manage Your Time, The 21 Irrefutable Laws of Leadership, The 21 Indispensable Qualities of a Leader,* and *The 100 Greatest Leadership Principles of All Time.*

The 'F' Word: Good Words for Great Leaders, offers a different perspective. First, it is a "quick" read, which for busy people may be a God-send. Second, there are only "7" words you need to remember. Third, the message applies to anyone regardless of title or station in life who wishes to inspire others. Finally, the book is designed to capture the human experience offering lessons from children, parents, executives, teachers, athletes, soldiers, nurses, volunteers, religious, and advocates for the common good.

"*Quo Vadis?*" The answer to that question depends on each person's ability to make right choices, concentrate on what's important, be faithful to one's responsibilities, be strong in adversity, accept difficult circumstances, forgive others, and believe in a higher power. Those who live and lead by these principles will not only know where they are going, but also who has chosen to follow them.

"F" WORD ONE

FREEDOM

> ***"Everything can be taken from a man but the last of human freedoms: to choose one's attitude in any given set of circumstances, to choose one's own way."***
>
> ***—Viktor Frankl***
> ***Auschwitz Survivor***

Bad Word … Good Words

Let's face it. The "F" word breeds discomfort. It gets a reaction. It crosses a line. It may have even prompted you to pick up this book. But there are other words that begin with the letter "F," words that are powerful in a more subtle way, that present positive challenges, that steer a conversation in a constructive direction. And should the topic of discussion include words like "freedom," "focus," "fidelity," "fortitude," "forgiveness," and "faith," then the conversation becomes really worthwhile. Even a word like "forbearance," though seldom used, has merit among those who recognize that the ability to delay gratification or accept difficult circumstances can be a good thing.

For those individuals who have leadership responsibility or wish to lead others, these seven "F" words represent all that is necessary to both inspire and succeed. To that end I invite all who have chosen to read this book to use these words (freedom, focus, fidelity, fortitude, forbearance, forgiveness, and faith) with confidence. But the choice is yours. That's why "freedom" is the first word that defines great leadership.

Everybody Does It

Why do some financial executives coach their accounting managers to "tweak" the numbers before the annual stockholder meeting? Is there a reason that certain baseball managers look the other way when a star player's performance is tied to steroid use? Should a school administrator genuflect to angry parents who claim their daughter's test was not fair or violation of the school's drinking policy does not warrant suspension?

In every case when a person in authority has a decision to make, he or she has been given a gift—freedom. They can take a stand, make the right choice, follow the rules, and ultimately do what is best for the greater good; or they can become complacent, knowingly make bad choices, bend those same rules and put their personal gain above what is best for their staff, organization, family, or community. Though today's leaders have the freedom to do what they feel is right, fair, and necessary, too many executives set bad examples for the next generation of management. They fail to demonstrate the courage needed to make *right* choices. Maybe that's why civility seminars for politicians, character education for students, and ethics courses for business men and women are in great demand. Even members of the military brass have added a "values" curriculum to basic training.

What was once expected appears to be the exception; or as one prophet said, "In 1960 there was a clear difference between a vegetarian and a cannibal. In the 21st century it is just a matter of taste!" And that recipe for poor leadership has five ingredients.

The Five Seductions

Seduction 1—Money: What accounts for the fact that some leaders are good while others other great? Are there certain traits or genes that seem to give one individual a significant advantage over another in the workplace, in the classroom, on the athletic field, or in society? Can you differentiate both classes of leadership by how much money people make, what they look like, how smart they are, what circles they run in, what privileges they receive, the power they wield, and what they indulge in?

If money is a key indicator of great leadership, how does one explain why so many wealthy executives find themselves in trouble with the law? Why do many professional athletes have agents who willingly sell their client's services to the highest bidder regardless of team loyalty? And who among us would wish to be "rich and famous" if it meant that our personal lives would be in shambles? Great leaders understand that it's not how much you earn that is important; rather, it's what you do with what you have. And the choices you make will ultimately define your legacy.

Seduction 2—Physical Presence: Two candidates for a television station anchor position were concerned that their chief competitor for the job (who had just walked out of the studio), was too good looking. In their minds, the search was over. Unfortunately for them, the gentleman who got the position had the most extensive experience, a better-sounding voice, and a commanding presence when he was on the air. And yes, he happened to be the best-looking finalist for the position. Nevertheless, his competition capitulated because they focused on one single attribute—looks—choosing to believe that there is a direct correlation between outstanding leadership and one's physical appearance. Apparently they never saw a picture of Abraham Lincoln.

Seduction 3—Intelligence: Having a high "intellect" is another attribute that gets too much credit for defining a great leader. It is one thing to graduate from an Ivy League university, quite another to be "street smart." There are many topnotch executives who admit that the best thing they ever did was to hire smarter people than themselves. I can think of no better example than the story of *Apollo 13* where hundreds of professionals all played a part in avoiding a space disaster. In the movie based on historical events, Ed Harris plays the role of Gene

Kranz, who was ultimately responsible for bringing astronauts Jack Swigert, Jim Lovell, and Fred Haise back safely to earth. Gene's faith in his Mission Control team gave him the confidence to declare in the face of possible disaster, "Not on my watch."

Seduction 4—Relationships: Relationships sometimes paint a misleading portrait. If a co-worker mentioned that she heard the new CEO had been married three times and didn't get along with his children, would that profile taint your first impression of the new boss? Or if another colleague provided evidence that the corporate board spoke highly of the new leader, would that information reverse your earlier opinion? Working relationships should be measured by direct encounters because great leaders judge others on what they know, not what others think they know.

Seduction 5—Power, Privilege, and Pleasure: There are those who believe that leadership should be measured by the three P's—power, privilege, and pleasure. Unfortunately history is filled with characters who had all three, but failed miserably. Some twentieth-century examples include Adolph Hitler, the architect of World War II whose actions resulted in the deaths of over 50 million; Idi Amin, the Ugandan dictator who is credited with the murder of over 300,000 of his own people; David Koresh, the leader of a branch of the Davidians who ultimately caused 84 deaths during a standoff with authorities in Waco, Texas; and Jim Jones, leader of the Peoples Temple who convinced 913 members to commit mass suicide in Guyana. These "leaders" had the freedom to make the right choice. They didn't and today their names live in infamy.

For those who believe that freedom comes without accountability, they would do well to listen to Janis Joplin's prophetic line from her famous song, "Me and Bobby McGee." The singer's haunting lyrics "Freedom's just another word for nothing else to lose," couldn't be further from the truth. And the truth is Janis Joplin died of a heroin overdose at age twenty-seven.

Freedom Lesson #1—The road to sorrow is littered with reputations of past leaders whose freedom to choose was clouded by poor vision and poor judgment.

It's All About Attitude

In Viktor Frankl's work, *"Man's Search for Meaning"* the author and clinical psychiatrist shared a number of stories about fellow prisoners he met at Auschwitz, the infamous concentration camp. One particular vignette caught my attention. It seems there was a prisoner who had a cheerful disposition regardless of the daily horrors he faced. As the man was dying, Frankl kneeled by his side and asked him how he could maintain such a positive outlook on life. The fellow inmate smiled and said that though his adversaries had taken his family, health, and dignity, they would never destroy his attitude.

As I read Frankl's description of this encounter, I began to think about the times in my own life when I had the freedom to choose an attitude contrary to what was expected. One particular event came to mind. I always had a policy that after reviewing an employee, I would turn the tables and invite that same staff member to give the boss *his* evaluation. At these discussions I often learned how I could improve our relationship or better support a member of my team.

During one of these sessions, an employee mentioned that members of the staff were a bit uncomfortable with my sense of humor. As he put it, "Because you're the boss you can joke with us in a manner that prohibits the staff from joking with you." I was very surprised at his comments, not to mention his refusal to recall a specific example.

Since he was the first person to receive the annual year-end review, I decided to test his hypothesis on the rest of the team during their evaluations. One by one I probed for behaviors that made the employee uncomfortable. There was no response. I asked more specific questions about my operating style. Again there was nothing to corroborate the first employee's remarks.

The following day I decided to give all my employees an opportunity to confirm or deny what was said of me by one of their colleagues. After a short meeting with the staff to cover the week's assignments, I retreated to my office, shut my door, and chose to remain unusually quiet for the entire day. When an employee needed to meet with me, I was polite but reserved. Near the end of the workday my executive assistant asked if she could talk with me for a few minutes. Janelle came in, shut the door, and said, "David, the entire staff is worried that perhaps you're not feeling well or somehow we have let you down." "Why would you think that?" I asked. She responded, "Because you're not yourself. You're too quiet and we miss your sense of humor." It was then I realized there was only one person who was uncomfortable with my management style—the same individual who purportedly spoke on behalf of the entire department. He had the freedom to accept who I was; And I had the freedom to be who I am.

Freedom Lesson #2—"Trust but verify" applies to both the arms and human race.

On another occasion I was the one that needed an attitude adjustment. As I was getting dressed one morning, I looked at my daily planner and realized I had several meetings that day guaranteeing another late night. On top of that, I knew I would be asked to facilitate a session between department heads whose performance was suffering because of their poor working relationship. And to add to my self-induced stress, I was concerned that several off-site meetings would curtail the day's productivity.

As a practicing Catholic I do my best to attend daily Mass before going in to the office. But on this particular morning, though it was difficult to drag myself to church, I decided to go and took a seat in the pew near the back. Unfortunately, I wasn't paying much attention to anything the priest said or did as I was too busy internally "whining" about the day ahead. There is a part in the Mass where everyone in attendance turns to those closest to them and offers some sign of peace. At that moment I shook hands with people on my right and left and mumbled some half-hearted salutation. Just then two teenagers in front of me turned around, looked at me, smiled, and said, "Peace be with you." In an instant I was mortified with my "woe-is-me" attitude as I found myself staring at a young boy and girl who (as I learned later) were in this country to receive plastic surgery on their tragically deformed faces!

Shame on me. Instead of thanking God for my health, job, family, and numerous other blessings, I chose to begin my day with a bad attitude. Worse yet, had I not encountered these two strangers my mental outlook would have surely infected everyone I came in contact with. Fortunately, I had the "freedom" to choose my disposition for the rest of the day. And what do you know, it turned out to be a pretty good day after all.

Freedom Lesson #3—No one ever choked on humble pie.

Shortly after that experience I received an email about another individual who had a similar "wake-up" call. This event occurred in a very ritzy area of Southern California. According to the message a young executive was driving his new Jaguar through a suburban neighborhood when suddenly he heard a "THUD!" on the passenger side of his car. Screeching to a halt he jumped out of his automobile and raced around the other side only to discover that his new Jag had just been hit with a brick. Looking quickly around, he saw a young boy standing a few feet away crying.

"Did you throw that brick?" the angry driver asked. "Yes sir," the boy stammered. "Son, you are in a lot of trouble!" At that moment the little boy pointed to another scene twenty feet away. There on the sidewalk was his brother whose wheelchair had tipped over pinning him to the ground. "You see, sir," the brick thrower continued, "I tried to get other drivers to pull over and help but no one would stop. And the only way I could get your attention was to throw a brick at your car." The owner of the Jaguar fell silent. He rushed over to lift the injured boy off the ground and place him back in his wheelchair

According to the email, the owner of the Jaguar never did fix the dent in his car. He wanted the experience to act as a reminder that there are things in life that need your immediate attention and it shouldn't take a brick to get this message across. He made a choice to treat the entire incident as a life-long learning experience. And because of his example, the story of one man's discernment will be repeated over and over again.

Freedom Lesson #4—It is better to give than to receive.

Freedom of Choice

Though everyone has the opportunity to make the "right" choice, that doesn't mean the courage to act accordingly comes easily. In my professional and personal life I have had the privilege to witness a number of scenarios where the person in power opted to take a "high road" approach for the greater good of the team, the organization, or the community they served. Jed was a towering first baseman who had played the position for over twenty years for the corporate services team. He was both well liked and respected by players and coaches. And though the years had taken their physical toll, he still could be counted on to make a dazzling defensive play, drive in the winning run, or pop for a round of beers after the game.

One spring a new player joined the team. He was twenty-five years younger than Jed, was a more consistent hitter, and played first base without the aches and pains that came with age. After a few scrimmage games it was clear that the team had to find a way to get the "young gun" in the lineup.

Just before the start of the season, Jed approached his long-time manager-friend and said, "Tom, it's time." "Time for what?" he inquired. Jed continued, "Tom, I'm going to hang up my cleats." The manager's jaw dropped. "But, Jed, I need you. The team needs you. Why are you doing this?" "Because, Tom, everyone knows that the new guy can more than do the job, and it would be unfair for this first baseman to take a position that rightly belongs to a younger player." Jed went on, "Besides, Bonnie and I were just talking the other day about finding the time to do more things together. That opportunity is now." And with those parting words Jed went over to the team and wished them well on their upcoming season.

Jed gave me two things that day. One was the opportunity to become the starting first baseman. More important, he gave me an outstanding example of how one should handle the situation when the time comes to say good-bye.

Freedom Lesson #5—"Class" is one gift everyone understands and wishes they had.

Chad is a very good friend of mine whose success as a small businessman is to be admired. As an investment consultant he often has the opportunity to work with young couples who look to him for advice.

One day a new client showed up for their first appointment. This man and his wife were in their mid-thirties and financially sound. As Chad was poring over their financial documents, he noticed the $120 dollar line-item that was recorded under charitable contributions. "I see you gave ten dollars a month to charity last year." Chad noted. "Yes, and I have the receipt," the lady responded with great enthusiasm. Chad went on, "Are there any other donations not recorded here?" "No, that's it," her husband responded.

With that Chad closed their books, looked at the couple and said, "I'm going to give you the best advice I can. And it's free." The pair looked intently at their new investment counselor. "I have been in business for over twenty years and every year I give more to charity than I did the previous year." Chad continued. "And funny thing, every year I make more money." Chad paused to see if his words had any effect. The silence was deafening. He made a final offer. "Think over what I just said. And next year if you want to use my services, give me a call." With that the young couple thanked Chad for his time and left.

I don't know if they ever returned to Chad's office. But I do know that both of them received a gift from an outstanding community leader whose personal return on investment is driven by a desire to help others.

Freedom Lesson #6—"You reap what you sow."

I have also had the privilege to work for three outstanding CEO's. The following stories reflect a wisdom common among great leadership.

John was often referred to as a "wise old fox." I learned why this label fit moments after he made me the offer to join his organization. "John," I asked, "I'm flattered that you would give me the opportunity to be part of your executive team, but why would you hire someone who has absolutely no experience in this industry?" "Son," he retorted, "you're not tainted." And to be sure that I remained that way his first assignment for the new Vice President of Marketing was to walk around for six months and come back and tell him what I learned.

On another occasion I was having trouble with a few physicians who had tried to undermine my hospital marketing strategy. I had all the evidence I needed to take my case before the CEO. The facts were on my side. Key members of both the medical and nursing staffs supported my position. And everyone knew I was justified protecting my turf. All of these points were spelled out in a letter addressed to my adversaries highlighting their bad behavior and self-serving attitudes.

I met with John to explain my grievance. After a brief discussion I shared the letter I intended to mail to the physicians. He read the letter, handed it back to me and said, "David, you are absolutely right. The doctors are wrong." He paused a moment and then continued. "But I'll tell you what I want you to do. Put the letter in your desk and keep it there for a day or two. When you're ready pull it out and read it again." His teaching continued. "If you still believe that mailing the letter is the best way to handle the matter, then send it. I will support whatever decision you make."

I never mailed the letter. I saved face. And the problem was solved because a great leader gave me the opportunity to make the right decision.

Freedom Lesson #7—Just because you are right doesn't mean you're right.

Bill was the kind of leader everyone wanted to be around. So when I received the call that he wanted to interview me for the position, Vice President of Planning and Marketing, I was flattered. His first request was easy: "David, tell me a little about yourself." I proceeded to talk about my chronological work experience supported by numerous documents designed to demonstrate that I offered what he was looking for. Five minutes into my "verbal" résumé, Bill said, "David, I believe your background is compatible with the needs of Children's Hospital. But what I'm really interested in is how you spend time with your family, what you do for your community, and what's important in life."

If I had said that I was responsible for increasing market share ten percent at the cost of spending time with my wife and children, the interview would have terminated. If I had communicated every detail in an award-winning advertising strategy, but failed to describe my volunteer commitment, Bill would have sent me packing. And if I had outlined my strategic planning process, with all its business acumen, but couldn't articulate life's priorities, I would never had spent ten years under the tutelage of one of the best-known child advocates in the country.

An additional point is worth noting. Before I was officially offered the position, Bill asked that my wife, Cindy, fly out to Akron, Ohio, to meet her husband's future boss. When Cindy returned from "her" interview, she said to me, "I don't know if Akron is a good place to raise a family, or if Children's Hospital is a good place to work; what I do know is that Bill loves children and that can't be all bad." As I look back, Bill was looking to hire a dedicated husband, father, and child advocate. And should that person have some background in marketing so much the better.

Bill's leadership taught me that there are more important things in life than credentials. And he gave me the freedom to both live and work accordingly.

Freedom Lesson #8—Résumés promise the past. Chemistry promises the future.

Denny offered a different lesson. When our number one competitor blitzed the marketplace touting their national quality rankings, our hospital was put in a very difficult position. And when their leading cardiac surgeon went on television and suggested that patients were six times more likely to die at our institution than his, our reputation suffered. From website to television spot, billboard to radio commercial, and through countless newspaper advertisements, the public was told that our competitor was the better choice for cardiac care.

And then it happened. One of our analysts discovered that the data used by the competing institution to compare their mortality rates with ours was wrong! A second review by a national organization confirmed that not only was our competitor using false information but our hospital had better quality indicators.

We had them. I couldn't wait to go public. My strategy called for a press conference with outside reviewers taking the lead to educate both the media and the community on which organization delivered the better care. Board members, leaders of the medical staff, nursing leadership, and other administrators were all willing to endorse a proactive approach that would embarrass the other community hospital.

But Denny chose a higher road. Working through multiple channels he convinced our adversary that it was in their best interest to remove all references to quality ratings. The billboards came down. Their website message changed. And print, radio, and television ads were pulled.

I tried to argue that had our competitor caught us in this position, they would have publicly ridiculed our organization. Denny's answer was humbling: "Yes, David, you're right. But what is best for the community is to avoid an all-out embarrassment of another hospital whose services are needed to care for our sick and injured citizens." Because of Denny's actions the story never broke. And I learned that when leaders are free to choose a greater good over self-serving agendas, everyone wins.

Freedom Lesson #9—In case you missed it: Just because you are right doesn't mean you're right.

Freedom: The First Principle for Great Leadership

So the choice is yours. You can follow the crowd and explain away bad decision making under the "everybody does it" dogma, or you can take the high road doing the right thing, at the right time, for the right reason. You can ignore others who desperately search for a role model, or you can step up and deliver the kind of leadership found among individuals who are known for their high moral character. You can whine that circumstances are unfair; or you can get to work and play the cards you have been dealt. You can hang on to "sacred cows" to the detriment of the organization and the people you serve; or swallow your pride and implement those changes required of great leadership. And finally, you can demand the freedom to do the job; or you can balance your request with the wisdom below:

"Freedom is only part of the story and half the truth. That is why I recommend that the Statue of Liberty on the East Coast be supplanted by a Statue of Responsibility on the West Coast."

Viktor Frankl

"F" WORD TWO

FOCUS

"You can't depend on your judgment when your imagination is out of focus."

—Mark Twain
American Author and Satirist

A Perfect "8"

"Perfection" is a wonderful word. Its very definition suggests something beyond excellent. Oh, if only it were possible in this life! Yet how many times have we tried to pick the perfect candidate? Be a perfect boss? Design the perfect product? Implement a perfect process? Choose a perfect opportunity? Marry a perfect spouse? Raise perfect children? Get the picture?

To achieve such heights, staff and leadership are often told that it's only a matter of "focus." If everyone would concentrate on the job at hand without letting little interruptions like human nature, competition, world events, or the common cold get in the way, success would be theirs.

But I would like to suggest a different interpretation of this often misunderstood attribute. To focus is the ability to adjust one's vision for purposes of greater clarity or productivity. The key word is vision. And if this gift allows us to see the whole picture, then the odds are the best candidate will be hired, the best attitude will surface, the best product will sell, the best protocol will be implemented, or the best opportunity will present itself. As for picking the best spouse or raising the best children, that is a little trickier.

There have been a number of people who have taught me what "to focus" really means. I begin with Michael. A number of years ago I had the opportunity to participate in a "search for family excellence" that allowed me to interview a number of outstanding families from around the country. One young gentleman was kind enough to send me a letter responding to questions regarding how well his parents raised him and his brothers. Specifically, I asked him how he would rate his parents if "10" were indeed perfect. The wisdom of his answer lowers the bar for all the right reasons.

Michael wrote: *I would have to give mom and dad about an "8" if "10" is perfect. A lot of times when the perfect thing to do would have been to say, "No, we can't afford it" they would say, "We'll see if there isn't some way we can work it out." There were times when they really had work to do but they took the time to play with me. They were not perfect, but then perfect people do not need love. It is their imperfections that make them special, that make them my parents. They are close enough to perfect for me.*

If my children echoed similar feelings at my eulogy, I would be the proudest resident in Heaven. Heck, if my staff said I was a perfect "8" because I did my best to work it out, or always found time to listen to their needs, dreams, concerns, and questions, that would be good enough for me.

Focus Lesson #1—The "8's" of this world are usually the ones who get things done. Besides, who wants to work with someone who is perfect?

Academic Leadership

As I previously mentioned, I have met some pretty outstanding parents. And one measure of their success was how they motivated their children to achieve in school. The following scenarios are representative of what happens when someone demands the best.

Kim was fourteen years of age and often struggled with her studies because of a learning disability. After interviewing her parents I asked permission to speak with their daughter. Her mother suggested I phrase my questions carefully so as not to confuse the teenager. I opened the conversation with a critical question. "What have been the best and worst of times with your parents?" After reflecting a few moments Kim finally said: "That question is so hard because my answer is the same." Figuring I failed to listen to her mother properly, I decided to break the question into two parts. Kim interrupted immediately. "No," she said, "I understand your question. You see, the worst of times with my parents is when they insist that I put that extra hour in my studies when all my friends are outside having fun." Kim continued, "But the best of times with my mom and dad is when I'm called up on stage to receive an academic award from the school that my parents were told would be too difficult for me."

David was the oldest of five children and very popular in high school. One Friday his mother received a call from the homeroom teacher informing her that her son was quickly becoming the "class clown." That evening Mom proudly announced that effective Monday morning, she would be joining David in class for the entire week and the empty desk behind his was reserved for her. "YOU'RE GOING TO DO WHAT?" he shouted. Calmly, David's mom explained that she had heard her son was quite popular and that it was her responsibility to transfer this "talent" to his younger brothers and sisters. Horrified at the prospect of his mother following him from class to class, David begged her to reconsider. Sensing desperation, she agreed to think it over for a week before she would initiate her plan to "shadow" her son. The following Friday afternoon the homeroom teacher called to alert David's mom that his behavior had taken a "remarkable" turn for the better. "It's a miracle," she replied.

Barry had a fourth-grade education and his wife barely finished eighth grade. Yet somehow this couple had inspired their children to become academic superstars. Dad's explanation was simple. "You see, when our children came home from school, the first thing we did was sit down as a family and have dinner." Barry continued, "After supper the kids knew to follow their dad into the study. Though I couldn't read, I still knew our encyclopedia set held a world of knowledge." Barry began to smile. "I would grab one of the volumes, open the book to no particular page, and ask all my children to read to their father." That was it; no special tutoring, computer software, or financial incentives. He just set an example and got the results he wanted.

Kim's parents taught their daughter how to focus on her studies. David's mom focused on her son's behavior. Barry focused on the importance of education by using the encyclopedia to foster a greater appreciation for learning. Though three different families used three different communication styles they all had one thing in common: the ability to focus.

Focus Lesson #2—Good leaders achieve the expected. Great leaders deliver the unexpected.

"Lord, That I May See."

Throughout my life there have been several individuals responsible for helping me assess a situation properly. Without their insight I would have surely missed the mark.

Sergeant Wheeler was the non-commissioned officer that most influenced me during my tenure with the United States Air Force. The year was 1969 and I was the chief dispatcher for air operations. In the evening I was the starting pitcher for the squadron's baseball team. During one of our games, Sergeant Wheeler came out to watch the base team battle an all-black club from Austin, Texas. He was one of the loudest cheerleaders in the stands as we proceeded to shut down their powerful offense. After the game I walked up to my supervisor and said, "Sarge, I appreciate your support but you've got to be careful." "What are you talking about?" he asked. After looking around to make sure no one would overhear our conversation, I continued. "Sarge, these are difficult times. Surely you noticed that all the players on our team are white, while all the players on their team, *like you*, are black." "So what?" he inquired with a note of irritation. I tried again. "Didn't you feel their fans staring at you when you were rooting for our team? I was afraid they were going to lynch you." Sergeant Wheeler began to laugh. "David," he said, "it's a wonder you won the game when you were so focused on your competitor's pigmentation." He was right.

Years later I was making a call on an advertising executive. I had never met this gentleman and knew little about him or his organization. Sitting outside his office, his secretary asked, "Have you ever met Mr. Anderson?" I explained that this was my first visit. At that she quietly said, "Well, let me prepare you. You are about to meet a monster." I was stunned. "Let me explain," the lady offered. "A few years ago Mr. Anderson and his wife were in a terrible car accident. She burned alive and he was horribly scarred for life." But she added, "Regardless, you will never meet a finer, more upbeat person." At that moment a voice on the intercom interrupted. "Peggy, has David arrived?" "Yes, Mr. Anderson, I'll send him right in." As she gestured to his office, I couldn't help but notice Peggy's comforting smile. I took a deep breath and proceeded to meet the "monster" on the other side of the door. He was standing behind his desk with his back to me gazing out of his third-story window. Without turning around he said, "David, have you ever seen a bad day?" Recalling his secretary's warning, I managed a timid response. "Well, sir, I believe we have all seen or experienced a bad day." "Come over here and I'll show you what a bad day looks like," he retorted.

Preparing for the worst I slowly walked toward the statuesque man. He turned and smiled with a face that was no more. "David," he said, "let me show you what a bad day looks like." He turned toward the window and pointed to the ground below. Adjacent to the office complex was a cemetery! "David," he continued, "now that's a bad day. You and I are about to have a good day." We did.

When Margaret from the American Marketing Association called and asked me to deliver a presentation having nothing to do with marketing, I was puzzled. "You see, David," she began, our next meeting falls on Valentine's Day and we have invited all our members to bring their spouse or significant other to enjoy the evening." Margaret went on. "And we heard about your 'Back to the Family' program and the humorous stories you tell about kids raising their parents." Given Margaret's specifications and the audience profile, I accepted the invitation. Moments before I began my keynote address, a marketing professor from the local university walked in with fifteen of his marketing students. "Uh-oh" I thought, are they going to be disappointed. After my presentation I was packing up my materials when I noticed that one of the students was heading my way. Here it comes, I thought; he came to the session to learn something about his chosen career and all I offered were stories about parents and their children. "Mr. Eich, do you have a moment?" he inquired. "Certainly," I said. "I want to thank you for your presentation this evening." "Thank you, but I'm sure you didn't learn much about marketing," I responded. "That's true," he replied. "But what you did is remind me that I haven't spoken with my parents in over three weeks. And that sad performance ends tonight!" I was humbled knowing that my words may have saved a relationship between a young man and the people who loved him most.

In the early '80s, one of the most popular television shows was "*The A Team*", starring George Peppard and a bouncer-like character known as Mr. T. Three of the team's greatest fans were my children. Every Tuesday evening Robbie, Andrew, and Kelly planted themselves in the family room prepared to experience another exciting adventure. One night Dad decided to channel surf during a commercial break. Progressing from one station to another I carelessly paused on a documentary detailing the horrors of the famine in Somalia. Images of starving children dominated the screen. Gathering my senses I attempted to return to *"The A Team"* only to be interrupted by my children's innocent voices. "Daddy, go back," they demanded. "What happened to those children? Why do they look so bad?" they asked. They wanted answers. "You see," I stammered, "they live in a faraway land and unfortunately they don't have money to buy enough food." "But what can we do to help, Daddy?" asked Robbie. "Can we send them food?" Andrew inquired. Before I could articulate an intelligent response, the program spokesperson invited "MY" children to feed "HIS" children. "Let's get our piggybanks!" Kelly yelled out. Moments later all three kids returned with their life's savings. And before the night was over, I was writing a check to cover my children's generosity and their father's personal shame. Mr. T would have been proud.

Focus Lesson #3—"Out-of-the-box" thinking makes others ask, "What was I thinking?"

The Search for Excellence

One of the greatest challenges leaders face is to find the right person to do the job. Traditional recruitment techniques, personal interviews, and reference checks guarantee nothing more than the peace of mind that comes from exercising due diligence. To increase the odds in your favor I might suggest that you focus your attention on two questions:

What makes them tick? And can they articulate why a favorable decision to hire them is the right choice?

To answer the first question, ask finalists to list their five most important things in life, in order, and why. There are three reasons for this inquiry. First, you want to see if the person you are considering for the position has his or her priorities in order. Their responses will typically tell you more about the character of the individual than any interview tool currently on the market. Second, can the candidate list each item immediately, or does it take a great deal of thought before the list is completed? If the former the odds are he or she is a very confident person who knows exactly where to focus his or her energy. And third, there is nothing illegal about the question. Either they know who they are or they don't. In one case I observed a 41-year-old nurse struggle with the question for several minutes until she finally admitted that the only thing she could list was music. She didn't get the job. On another occasion I had two outstanding candidates for a position and figured that the "tie-breaking" question would give the nod to the better applicant. Much to my surprise, both candidates listed EXACTLY the same five priorities in EXACTLY the same order! I almost flipped a coin to see who would get the offer.

To answer the second question, invite each finalist to write a letter postdated three years in the future that justifies the decision you made to hire them three years earlier. Unlike the traditional "Where do you see yourself in 'X' years" question, candidates are challenged to list accomplishments they will achieve in the coming three years that will be of value to you and the organization. It's a stern test. Some individuals struggle because they have little or no vision. Others don't like being accountable for a job they haven't been hired for. But there are applicants whose courage paints a picture that may allow you to better discern which candidate is best for the job. These interview questions offer additional tools that go beyond paper qualifications you had nothing to do with, references from people you don't know, and metaphysical "chemistry" that often blows up in the human lab.

Diamonds in the Rough

If there's one thing youth baseball coaches learn, it's that the ground ball between the legs, the called strike three, and the game-ending dropped fly ball are long forgotten moments after the taste of ice cream. On the ball diamond there are more opportunities to teach others how to focus than in any other venue. And sometimes the coach is the student. The following stories prove my point.

Brandon was a little boy from Brazil who had beautiful brown eyes. While he was standing on first base, his coach leaned over and said, "Brandon, on the next pitch I want you to steal." "Got it, Coach," the confident ten-year-old responded. The pitch was on its way when Brandon broke for second base. But for some reason he stopped halfway to the bag. "Brandon," I yelled, "get back to the base." By now the other team's entire infield was chasing my player as he desperately ran for his life. "You're out!" yelled the umpire. The inning was over. The game was over. And one sad little boy stood mystified as to what he had done or failed to do. I put my hands on his little shoulders and asked, "Brandon, what happened?" Looking up at me with tears welling in his eyes, he said, "Coach, I'm sorry, I guess I'm just a little boy who got confused." An hour later we both enjoyed a large dish of chocolate ice cream—guaranteed to remind both of us what was important in life.

Louie was the perfect example of why each coach decides to hide his worst player in right field. The hope is that no harm will come his way. But one particular Saturday morning, predestination helped my player make a career decision. With our team winning by one run I almost had a heart attack when I saw the fly ball heading in Louie's direction. I shouted, "Louie, have you got it?" "I got it, Coach," he responded. PLUNK! The ball hit Louie squarely in the head. I'm not sure who ran faster: Louie's coach to check the damage or the player who hit the tying home run off my right fielder's skull. "Louie, are you all right, son?" I asked. My brave right fielder (much to my chagrin) stood up, wiped away a few tears, and proudly declared, "I'm ok, Coach. I can still play." With parents cheering for Louie there was nothing I could do but pray that this would never happen again—especially with the score tied in the last inning. Alas, fate can be unkind. The very next batter saw an opportunity and proceeded to send another fly ball in Louie's direction. "LOUIE, have you got this one?" He looked up, looked at me, and said, "Sorry, Coach, but I'm outta here." With that declaration my most famous right fielder ran off the field to protect his remaining brain cells. We lost the game and beloved Louie gave up his baseball career to become a physician.

Focus Lesson #4—Wisdom sometimes hides itself in another's decision to abandon what you think is important.

Andrew is my second-born son whose personality was best summed up by another parent who said, "You have just got to love that boy. Thank God he's yours!" Nevertheless, as his father I was confident that he could differentiate between my dual role as coach and dad. To that end, I initiated a critical father/son conversation on the way to the first game of the season. "Son," I began, "as you know we are going to play the toughest team in our division. And that's why I've decided to put you in the lineup as our starting pitcher." "Yup," he replied while looking out the window and chewing on a piece of gum that must have weighed two pounds. I continued, "And because this is the best hitting team in the league, you are probably going to give up more than a few runs." "Yup," my ballplayer/son said proving that one-syllable words can be effective. "And finally, Andrew, if the *coach* decides to pull you out of the game because you're getting pounded, I don't want any lip. Is that clear, son?" "Yup," said the future public speaker. Andrew took the mound and proceeded to strike out twelve consecutive batters. After facing the last hitter in a 13–0 blowout, Andrew walked off the mound, turned to me, winked, and said, "How's that, Dad, I mean, Coach?"

Focus Lesson #5—Never assume that little or no response means that someone isn't listening.

Though children do a terrific job teaching coaches, parents, and other adults how to focus, there are ample opportunities to share the same wisdom with the kids.

Sean was a terrific pitcher. And his greatest fan was his mom, who had the curious habit of downing three antacids every time her son took the mound. One day Sean was having control problems that allowed the opponents to cut our lead to one run. I knew that if he just got the ball over the plate the opposing batters couldn't hit him. Just before I walked out to have a conference with my player, I turned to Roxanne and said, "When you see me walking out to talk with your son, I want you to come down to the bench and walk right up to the foul line. Don't step on the field; just be visible so he can see you out of the corner of his eye." Mom nodded and was ready to play her part. I strolled out to the mound. "Sean," I asked, "what's the problem?" "I dunno, Coach, I just can't seem to throw strikes." I noticed that his attention was drifting over my right shoulder. "Well, son, here's what I'm going to do. If you walk one more batter, I'm going to send your mother out here to take you out of the game." Sean nearly fainted. "Coach, you can't do that," he said, picking up Roxanne's glare. "If you don't want that to happen, all you have to do is throw the ball over the plate." With that I turned around and walked back to the bench. Roxanne returned to her seat to check the antacids inventory. Sean's next nine pitches were right down the middle as he notched three consecutive strikeouts. Roger Clemens couldn't have done any better.

As a baseball manager who has coached over 500 youth baseball games, I am proud to say that I was never ejected. I was, however, brought up on charges by parents of an opposing team. During one particular season our team was by far the class of the league. As we were well on our way to an undefeated record, I continually warned my team to never let their guard down as any club on any given day could knock us from our perch. My message fell on deaf ears during a game with an opponent that had won only three of their fifteen games. "C'mon, Coach," my players chanted, "There is no way we are going to lose to the Bears." They were right. We won the game in extra innings because one of their players made a costly error. After the game my team was deathly quiet. Their moms and dads were steaming. And my assistant coach, Ed, was preparing to get their attention. "Oh, boys," Ed began, "since you were too tired to hustle during the game, your coach has decided that perhaps a little exercise will wake you up. Ed directed the ballplayers to third base where wind sprints would be the educational tool of choice. That was the last time the team took anyone for granted, failed to prepare before the game, or neglected to play hard during a game. Ironically the parents of the other team felt that I was abusing the kids, while our own parents totally supported the lesson plan. We finished the season undefeated.

Focus Lesson #6—The choice is simple: pay attention and focus, or be the focus of unwanted attention.

Focus: The Second Principle for Great Leadership

Mark Twain began this chapter by stating, "You can't depend on your judgment when your imagination is out for focus." There is, however, a proverb that says, "Think of many things. Do only one." On the surface it would seem that there is somewhat of a dichotomy between the two statements. Twain appears to suggest that you must allow all kinds of thoughts to impact your decision. The author of Proverbs cautions the reader to avoid distractions. For my money, I believe both interpretations complement each other. Great leaders recognize that the need to "focus" is a critical attribute for success. But they also recognize that creativity properly mixed with managerial discipline is the best of both worlds.

"F" WORD THREE

FIDELITY

"Many persons have a wrong idea of what constitutes true happiness. It is not attained through self-gratification but through fidelity to a worthy purpose."

—Helen Keller
American Memoirist and Advocate for the Blind and Deaf

For Better or Worse

To be faithful to one's family, organization, or country is expected. When we sign a contract, we make a commitment to live up to its terms. When we stand at the altar across from our future spouse, the vows we repeat is our promise to remain at that person's side regardless of what lies ahead. And should our nation fall under attack everyone is expected to do his or her part. Loyalty to your loved ones, staff, the boss, teammates, and those neighbors, friends and colleagues whom you depend on is an ideal to shoot for.

Unfortunately fidelity, though noble in principle, is under siege. When employees are caught trying to sell trade secrets to competitors, when husbands and wives abandon each other and their children, when professional athletes "sell their souls" to the highest bidder, and when men and women in all occupations and leadership positions use bad judgment, many people are hurt.

All of us have had the opportunity to observe what "fidelity" means and how it impacts others. Many of us have our own story to tell. And some of us have been exposed to examples, both good and bad, that demonstrate why this "F" word is a mandatory leadership trait. The stories that follow underline the differences between loyalty and betrayal.

A Special Victory ... A Devastating Defeat

A number of years ago a story was circulating out of Seattle that during the Special Olympics the crowd witnessed something rarely seen in athletic competition. Nine children with various handicaps were ready to run a 100-yard dash. The starter fired the gun and all the contestants began their journey down the track. Forty or so yards into the race, a girl who was leading the competition looked back and noticed that one of the boys had fallen. She stopped running as did her fellow racers. Suddenly, all eight children ran back to their fallen comrade, helped him up, locked arms, and continued to run in unison until they all crossed the finish line together. The nine children stood in the winner's circle with their arms raised celebrating their victory. There was hardly a dry eye in the stadium. For these children "winning" was "caring."

In the state of Ohio a different team also wanted to win. They were ahead by one run in the last inning of a fifteen-year-old state championship baseball game that would determine which club would go to the nationals. With only one out away from victory, the opposing batter hit a hanging curveball for a triple. There were still two outs. The next batter hit a one-hop ground ball back to the mound where the pitcher cleanly fielded the ball. Instead of throwing to first base to end the game and propel his team into the national spotlight, he tried to throw the runner on third out at the plate. The throw was high. The runner was safe. The score was tied. Meanwhile, the runner at first base scampered down to second. The next batter singled up the middle scoring the winning run from second base. The losing players, their fans, and coaches were devastated. The pitcher on the mound was crying for he knew that it was his mental error that ended a dream. Regardless, every player on his team went up to him and did his best to comfort a fellow teammate. The compassion shown to the broken-hearted pitcher was one of the best examples of sportsmanship I have ever witnessed. The following year, however, the coaches and players learned that the same boy whose team stood behind him in his darkest hour had chosen to play for a rival club.

A Family Christmas ... A Lonely Birthday

Sherry was the very "spirit" of Christmas. From decorating the house, to wrapping gifts, from baking cookies, to singing carols, it was her time to orchestrate the holiday season celebrations with her husband and six children. But one year, Sherry was suffering from a severe back injury necessitating multiple painkillers and mandatory bed rest. She felt that she was letting her family down. Depression was approaching as each day moved closer and closer to December 25.

On Christmas Eve, Dad called his children together around the "poorly" decorated tree. "Look, kids," he started, "Mom is very sad because she can't do what she has always done for us at Christmas time." He went on. "I think our job is to bring Christmas to your mother." A plan was crafted to be executed the moment Mom fell asleep. Two hours later everything was in place. The tree was moved upstairs and positioned so that Mom would see the masterpiece as soon as she woke up. The manger scene was set up on the night stand. Presents were competing for bedroom floor space. And candles were lit while "Silent Night" was softly playing in the hallway. The children stood around Mom's bed, quietly waiting for her to awaken. Dad was alone in the corner, moved by the outpouring of his children's love for their mother. As Sherry began to arouse from her slumber, the children whispered in unison, "Merry Christmas, Mom." Dad followed with a tearful, "Merry Christmas, Honey." A few years later the children were asked in an interview to identify the best times they had with their mom. They cheerfully responded, "It was the year we gave Mom Christmas."

In a Florida newspaper I came across an anonymous letter to the editor that told a different story:

Yesterday was an old man's birthday. He was 91. He awakened earlier than usual, bathed, shaved, and put on his best clothes. "Surely they would come today," he thought. He didn't take his daily walk to the gas station to visit with the old-timers of the community because he wanted to be right there when they came. He sat on the front porch with a clear view of the road so he could see them coming. Surely they would come today. He decided to skip his noon nap because he wanted to be up when they came. He has six children. Two of his daughters and their married children live within four miles. They hadn't been to see him for such a long time. But today was his birthday. Surely they would come today. At suppertime he refused to cut the cake and asked that the ice cream be left in the freezer. He wanted to wait and have dessert with them when they came. About 9 o'clock he went to his room and got ready for bed. His last words before turning out the lights were, "Promise to wake me up when they come." It was his birthday and he was 91.

A Mother's Joy ... A Son's Sorrow

On January 3, 1970, a sixteen-year-old Miami girl named Edwarda lapsed into a diabetic coma. Moments before this happened, she turned to her mother and pleaded, "Promise you won't leave me, will you, Mommy?" Such is the story of Kaye O'Bara, the mother who for over thirty-seven years has remained at her daughter's side cleaning her, feeding her, changing her, praying for her, and loving her. Through the years friends, family members, medical experts, and local authorities have asked Kaye why she refuses to "pull the plug" and let nature take its course. She simply says, "I asked God for two daughters, and I didn't put restrictions on it." Kaye goes on, "Besides, pity kills people." Kaye's devotion to her daughter is best described in inspirational author Wayne Dyer's book *A Promise is a Promise*. The title of Mr. Dyer's work is as good a definition for "fidelity" as one will ever see.

A few years ago my wife and I sent our oldest son, Robbie, to a high-school sponsored retreat. Parents were strongly advised to be in attendance that Friday evening when the students returned from their four-day emotional experience. At the closing ceremony each student walked up to the podium and publicly thanked their parents for all they had done for them. Gratefulness, reconciliation, and hope were common themes. After looking for his mom and dad and realizing they were not in attendance, one senior decided to change his speech. He began, "This retreat helped me understand what I need to do to have a better relationship with my parents. Predictably, they are too busy to listen to what I have to say." With that he walked off the stage. That night happy parents welcomed their sons and daughters home. But for one young man, his estranged journey would continue.

Fidelity Lesson #1—Be haunted by what you did or failed to do; or bask in the glory that you did the right thing, at the right time, for the right reason.

Fidelity School

There are a number of fidelity courses of study open to those who wish to become a great leader. The first of these is parenthood. During the eighteen-year plus curriculum moms and dads will encounter numerous scenarios that will test their resolve to love their kids unconditionally. And during this training parents will also learn that children are remarkable teachers.

When our three-year-old son Andrew kicked out the basement window moments before the moving van arrived, Mom had to remind herself that he was only a child who didn't understand that playing the "Karate Kid" with property we no longer owned wasn't a good idea. Robbie's explanation that he was only the "guard" during a massive egg-throwing demonstration was an interesting test for both child and parents. And Kelly's innocent misunderstanding that the VCR was not a TOASTER—which ultimately cost $50 per slice of bread—taxed even the best of parents. Fidelity lesson plans increase in intensity as children become adolescents and teenagers become young adults. It doesn't stop there. The time will come when your grandchildren join the faculty.

A second fidelity course is open for those who wish to learn from the workplace. When it came to motivating others, Les was a master of manipulation. When he called the "first-ever" professional sales training program for representatives who were accountable to no one, the whining was deafening. Why did they have to learn selling techniques when they were already successful? What value was there in a two-week training program that pulled them out of the marketplace? And who did this guy think he was anyway? On the first day of mandatory attendance one could feel the tension in the room as the new Vice President of Sales and Marketing stood before his class. "Welcome," Les began. "I know that many in this room would rather be working back home. I understand that." And then he made them a promise. "By this time tomorrow I'm confident that all of us will be on the same page." The next day a strange metamorphosis took place as every person in the room was engaged in the day's discussions. It was later that I learned that Les had sent flowers to the wives of every representative attending the program. With the flowers he attached the following note: "I want to personally thank you for allowing me the privilege to both train and inspire your husband. Your sacrifice will be rewarded in the near future. Best wishes, Les." Over time the loyalty and respect for this man became legendary.

Helen was another leader who had a knack for engaging her staff. As the new Vice President for Nursing at a major Midwestern hospital, she was responsible for over 700 clinical professionals. Her initial challenge was to address a serious morale problem among nursing ranks. The first day she started, Helen called in her executive assistant and requested that over the next ten days every supervisor be scheduled thirty minutes to personally meet the new nursing officer. Around-the-clock meetings were held with over eighty personnel. No conversation was off limits. Some nurses shared their anger, others cried, and almost everyone opened up with what was right and wrong about the organization. Within two weeks this remarkable woman had won the respect of the entire nursing force. There were a number of reasons for her success. Helen listened. Helen was professional. And Helen had a great sense of humor. Add these three traits together and you have a foundation for building trust. And trust is fidelity's cornerstone.

A third course provides lessons from movies, books, or personal encounters with others. Arguably the best movie ever made was *It's a Wonderful Life,* starring Jimmy Stewart as George Bailey. The leading character was the son of a man who founded the "Bailey Savings & Loan" in a fictional town named Bedford Falls. It was in this little community that George experienced happiness and despair. When he was ready to travel the world, his dad suddenly died forcing him to take over the family business until his younger brother, Harry, returned from college. When Harry returned the new graduate had already signed a contract to work in another city. Once again George was stranded in Bedford Falls. Later as George was preparing to leave on his honeymoon, he received word that the family business was about to go under. He used all the money in his savings to salvage the institution. And when his uncle misplaced a large sum of cash from the business, George realized that he, his uncle, or both would be arrested for embezzlement.

But the story of George Bailey really began when his guardian angel, Clarence, stopped him from committing suicide. George eventually came to understand how much good he had done in his life through a series of flashbacks that showed what life would have been like for many people in Bedford Falls if George had "never been born." Harry would have drowned because George was not there to rescue him. The town's pharmacist would have landed in prison because George was not around to catch a deadly prescription error. Mary, George's wife, would have lived a lonely life as an "old maid." His uncle would have become an alcoholic and the family business would have gone bankrupt because George was not there to manage both. At the end of the movie, George begs God to "let him live again." His sorrow eventually turns to joy as family, friends, and Bailey Savings & Loan customers unite to save the man who never abandoned them.

Another movie that communicates what's important in life is *The Greatest Game Ever Played*, the true story about Francis Ouimet, the twenty-year-old golf amateur who won the 1913 U.S. Open Championship. Though the event revolved around the unbelievable competition between Francis and British professionals Harry Vardon and Ted Ray—two of the best players in the world—the subplot centered on the relationship Ouimet had with his ten-year-old caddy, Eddie Lowery. As the contest headed to the final day, it was clear that young Francis was America's only hope to win the tournament. On that last day tour officials tried to get Francis to dump his caddy for a "more professional" assistant. To Francis' credit he resisted the pressure to relieve Eddie of his duties. His loyalty to the young boy who carried the future champion's clubs was a testament to fidelity.

On a more personal experience I had the opportunity to interview a remarkable lady and her son, Ronnie. Mary shared the challenges she faced caring for a teenager that had Tourette's syndrome, a severe neurological disorder characterized by multiple facial and body tics, grunts and compulsive utterances, and obscenities. After talking with this single parent for over three hours, she asked if I would care to interview her son. Before he sat down Mary cautioned me that she could not predict his behavior, especially in an unfamiliar setting that might trigger his anxiety. Ronnie was a big strapping boy with an infectious smile. Mom introduced me, and Ronnie reached for my hand. All seemed to be going well. But the moment I turned the tape recorder on he shook his head violently, cursed, and tried to kick me. Seconds later he calmed down. During our conversation there were moments of high anxiety for everyone in the room. When I got to a question about the best of times with his mother, Ronnie seemed to experience a totally different disposition. He looked at her lovingly, smiled, and said, "The best of times with my mom are when we both kneel down at night to pray, so that I can face tomorrow." At that moment I witnessed the gift of fidelity through a mother's faithfulness to her son, and a son's love for his mother.

Fidelity Lesson #2—If you touch their heart, they will remember your soul.

Till Death Do Us Part

"For better or worse, for richer or poorer, in sickness and in health, till death do us part" was my personal guarantee that I was willing to stick with Cindy in good times and bad. I promised to love her even when she gave me reason not to. My vow would demand that I have the courage to forgive and the humility to know when I needed forgiveness. And most of all, my "I Do" was a public tapestry that would display how faithful I would be to my wife.

Everyone knows that marriage is hard work. And though I was fortunate to marry my childhood sweetheart—the same girl who sent me a letter every day for two-and-a-half years while I was in the service—I still almost lost her because of my self-serving drive to get ahead. I had to complete my education. I had to work full time. I had to play ball on weekends with my friends. I had to be happy. But something happened on my hedonistic journey.

I had just received a promotion at General Motors in their Fisher Body Division. It was my first day in my new assignment. Early afternoon I felt a slight twinge of discomfort on my left side. As the workday ended I headed off to class where I was studying for my master's degree. That evening the pain increased. By the time class ended I was nearly bent over in agony. Somehow I managed to drive home. When I arrived on the doorstep, Cindy took one look at me and said, "David, you don't look well."

The following morning all "hell" broke loose. I was in severe pain and had projectile vomiting. My wife rushed me to the hospital where for the next five days I had every diagnostic test known in the medical world. I kept thinking about my job, classes, and of course softball season. Cindy had other things on her mind as there was the distinct possibility that her husband of three years was dying of cancer! There was a serious disconnect and I was the reason for the malfunction.

On the sixth day, a surgeon came into my room. "David," he began, "I've got to be honest with you. We don't know why you are so sick. But what we do know is you have poison in your blood stream." I lay there in silence waiting for my death sentence. Cindy was crying. The doctor continued. "Tomorrow we're going to open you up and determine what's causing your illness." With that he left the room.

When you are twenty-five years old lying in a hospital bed with your young wife weeping at your side, you suddenly begin to realize that perhaps there are more important things in life than your personal agendas. Class assignments no longer mattered. The loss of an entire semester was irrelevant. My new job would have to wait. And as for my team, well most of the guys had already written me off for the season. All that was left was all that was important: Cindy.

"Gangrene? But how? Why?" I demanded to know. "Frankly, David, no one on the medical staff has a clue" was the doctor's response. "All I can say is that you're a lucky young man because your wife brought you in when she did, and now that same lady is ready to nurse you back to health." His words stung my soul. The Cindy I had no time for had been at my side for seven straight days. My wife had honored our marriage vows. The only question remaining was whether or not I would keep my end of the bargain.

As I look back on my "darkest" hour, I now know that God sent me a physical cross to carry at a time in my life when I was jeopardizing my marriage. Since then, I have put my priorities in order. As a result, Cindy and I will soon celebrate four decades together.

Fidelity Lesson #3—Fidelity is not reserved for the best; rather, it is for those who can honestly say they did their best.

Semper Fi

This Latin phrase meaning, "Always Faithful" is the popular motto of the United States Marine Corps. It is also the accepted motto for no fewer than four other military groups from around the globe. The call-to-action can also be found in the literature promoting a fraternity, an English soccer club, and a high school.

There is another group that "lives" the meaning 24 hours a day, 365 days a year. Those gentlemen that watch over the *Tomb of the Unknown Soldier* are a special group of dedicated soldiers who follow rigid standards in the line of duty. They must fall within certain height and weight limits, live two years in special accommodations beneath the tomb, avoid alcohol or swearing, and study the lives of those laid to rest in Arlington National Cemetery.

Their commitment to duty was best exemplified when Hurricane Isabelle approached the shores of Washington, D.C. in 2003. City politicians and government workers took two days off to avoid the wrath of the storm. But when the tomb's guards were given permission to suspend their assignment, every man in the unit refused to abandon his post. Because of their fidelity to duty, the *Tomb of the Unknown Soldier* has been guarded around the clock for over seventy-five years. Their example sets a very high bar for what it means to be faithful to one's obligations. And you can bet that these men will one day set the same high standards when they are called to lead others.

Fidelity: The Third Principle of Great Leadership

To be faithful to one's obligations is a first step. But to be a role model for those in your charge while executing your duties is equally important. Those who wish to aspire to become great leaders must achieve both. When children see their mom and dad doing what it takes to keep the family together, they have someone they can emulate when the time comes for them to raise a family. When employees see their manager set the standard for hard work, integrity, and fairness, they have the tools they need to treat others as they would want to be treated. When the team captain takes the lead to deal with adversity, his fellow players have the blueprint necessary to face similar challenges. When a community leader demonstrates a willingness to remove political barriers, the people will rally around her. And when the CEO chooses to sacrifice personal gain for the greater good of the company *and* its employees, a standard has been set that will define the legacy of his leadership. In the end, everything will be measured by how faithful one is to that "worthy purpose" Helen Keller spoke about at the beginning of this chapter.

"F" WORD FOUR

FORTITUDE

> ***"A man's word and his intestinal fortitude are two of the most honorable virtues known to mankind."***
>
> ***—Jim Nantz***
> ***CBS Sportscaster***

Leadership Menus

There is a lot of help out there for those who wish to improve their leadership skills. You can go to the bookstore and order over 22,000 books with the word "leadership" in the title. If you prefer the "self-help" section, 38,000 volumes await. If "character" is your area of concentration, then you have another 31,000 to choose from. If a spiritual leadership trip is on your agenda, then you have 8,000 books to consider. Ethics, morals, virtues, and values offer over 20,000 additional choices.

And if reading isn't your preferred method of learning, then there are thousands of CD's and DVD's to purchase not to mention an untold number of leadership seminars you can attend.

With so many "experts" telling you how to be a good leader, is it any wonder that there are conflicting management styles? Dr. Ray Guarendi, author and clinical psychologist, often talks about "parenting facts of life." As I read his "common sense" tenets for parenthood, I couldn't help but notice the similarities between parents and leaders. For those that have the dual responsibility of raising children and inspiring adults, I think they will find the following advice mutually compatible.

Parenting Fact of Life #1—There are no perfect parents (leaders). Strong parents (leaders) don't have all the answers and don't always know what to say or how to say it.

Parenting Fact of Life #2—Mistakes are as integral to the home life (workplace) as children (employees) are. Strong parents (leaders) don't fear mistakes.

Parenting Fact of Life #3—Parents (leaders) aren't always paragons of patience. Patience is an ideal to strive for. It is not a day-to-day reality.

Parenting Fact of Life #4—Parents (leaders) aren't always popular. Strong parents (leaders) may be temporarily disliked because they are willing to make decisions based on their family's (company's) long-term welfare.

Parenting Fact of Life #5—Time is the essence of the home life (workplace) and the framework for investing in the family's (company's) greatest resource—its children (people).

As I studied these parenting/leadership "facts of life," it became clear that "fortitude" is what differentiates good parenting from great parenting—good leadership from great leadership. Demanding perfection won't cut it. Learning from your mistakes will. "Patience" like "tolerance" has its place. The key is having the fortitude to know when, and when not, to act. Right decisions won't define popularity. It will define courage. And as for time, it's the one investment where you truly "reap what you sow."

Stupidity or Courage?

The road to leadership is often filled with provocative potholes designed to challenge convictions. The following confrontations are two examples where my "intestinal" fortitude was enough to upset my intestines.

Example—1: Colonel Cycoski was a no-nonsense commander who expected excellence in the air operations group. Training was precise. Policies were followed. Professionalism was expected. Dispatchers were trained to launch "broken arrow" base inspections, handle aircraft crashes, and oversee Air Force 1 protocols. And no pilot, regardless of rank or reputation, would have a flight plan filed without the authorization of a member of our team.

One Sunday morning a pilot came into "base ops" to test fly a T-33 trainer jet. Major Denning approached the operations desk and handed me his proposed flight plan. "Major Denning," I started, "the colonel has instituted a new policy that every pilot must date and sign the card that shows you are authorized to take the plane up for a flight test." The major glared at me. "Sergeant, do you know what day it is?" he asked. "Yes, sir, it's Sunday." The officer continued. "Since you are keenly aware of both the day and the hour, then you must also be aware that I'm mad as hell that I have to give up my day off to fly this plane." "Sir," I responded, "I'm sorry for your inconvenience but I cannot file your flight plan unless you sign the attached card." Major Denning's face turned beet red. "*SERGEANT, YOU FILE THIS FLIGHT PLAN OR I WILL HAVE YOUR ASS!*" he shouted.

I now had a little dilemma. If I filed the flight plan, Colonel Cycoski would have more than my rear end for not following procedure. If I refused the major's demand, he would report me for disobeying a direct order. In effect I was put in a position where I had to choose the "lesser of two evils." I picked up the security police phone hoping my action would not get me busted. "Corporal James, speaking." "Corporal, this is Sergeant Eich in base ops. I want an armed guard stationed in front of the T-33 and advise them they have the green light to use whatever force is necessary to stop any pilot who does not have authorization to fly the aircraft. Is that clear, corporal?" "You got it," my friend in security police responded. Had Major Denning been armed I'm sure I wouldn't be telling this story.

Seconds later, a military police jeep pulled up in front of the plane. Two airman with side arms jumped out of the vehicle and took immediate positions to ensure that no one was about to steal a United States military aircraft. "YOU SONOFABITCH! I WILL HAVE YOUR STRIPES!" Denning screamed. I quietly handed the major a pen and said, "Sir, your signature or your life." He signed the card and threw it at me along with his flight plan.

That Monday morning I was called into Colonel Cycoski's office. He listened to my story and then dismissed me. The only feedback I got about the incident came from Master Sergeant Wheeler who said, "You did what was right and so did the colonel."

Example—2: Fifteen years later I had just started my new job in Omaha, Nebraska, working for a major tertiary care hospital. I was the first marketing executive to ever hold the position. That was both good and bad. On the bright side, I had an opportunity to do what had never been done before at this well-known institution. On the other hand, some physicians welcomed my discipline the way they would have received a used car salesman while certain administrators tried to convince the CEO that there was no need to hire an outsider.

I had been on the job for less than six weeks when the chief nursing officer pulled me aside and said, "David, you need to know that certain members of administration have purposely excluded you from meetings you should be attending." She went on. "Further, they are planting 'seeds' that you can't be trusted." After a brief conversation I decided to confront my potential adversaries. I scheduled a private session with the foundation officer and his two direct reports, one responsible for planning and the other for public relations. "Gentlemen," I began, "it has come to my attention that my performance has been called into question." I looked directly at the three men sitting across from me. "To that end, would you please outline for me all that I have done or have failed to do?" One accusation after another flew across the table. I was busy taking notes, refusing to comment one way or another.

At the end of their diatribe I put my pen down and said, "Frankly I'm very surprised at your list of complaints. But rather than try to defend my actions, I think it would be better to bring this matter directly to the attention of the CEO." The response was immediate. "What do you mean?" my counterpart demanded to know. "Well," I started, "since I have been here less than two months and the organization has invested a fair amount of money in my recruitment, it's only fair that if in fact I'm not doing the job then hospital leadership needs to know." With that I got up and left the room proceeding directly to administration. The foundation officer quickly followed. [Note: This tactic is only recommended for those in leadership positions who are young, inexperienced, and a bit naïve.]

The CEO was sitting behind his desk. "John," I began, "sorry to interrupt your morning but I thought you should be aware that I just had a conversation with Ben and his two directors regarding my performance." I handed him the list. "I made these notes during the meeting." The foundation officer was silent. At this point it occurred to me that I had directly challenged a fellow administrator who had over ten years seniority. A further complication was the reality that to do my job effectively I had to work with all three antagonists.

John looked up and said, "Ben, what's going on here?" It was my turn to remain silent. "John," Ben stammered, "I don't know what my directors were thinking, but I'll speak with them." I wasn't sure if the CEO caught my sideway glance, but I was sure he didn't like Ben's answer to his question. "Ben," John asked a second time, "what's going on?" To my astonishment Ben repeated the exact same answer. John looked at us for what seemed like an eternity. He finally spoke. "Gentlemen, let me sleep on this matter. I'll get back to both of you in the morning." With that we departed down opposite sides of the hallway.

It was a long night. I kept playing the scenario over and over again in my head. One moment I criticized my handling of the situation; the next moment I rationalized that I had to take a stand. The following morning the CEO called me into his office. Ben's absence was unsettling. "David," he began, "effective immediately the director of public relations is now reporting to you. John went on. "I'll inform Ben of my decision. Thank you for bringing this matter to my attention."

That was it. There was no further conversation. I was greatly relieved. That was not the case with the director of public relations who almost had a heart attack when he found out that his new boss was the same guy he tried to hang twenty-four hours earlier. Two and a half years later I was recruited by Children's Hospital Medical Center of Akron. Before I left Omaha, I made a strong pitch to the CEO to give my young director the opportunity to fill my shoes.

Looking back, the gift of fortitude gave me the courage necessary to survive the political showdown, and the same attitude was responsible for the success of the director of public relations who eventually became the vice president of marketing.

Fortitude Lesson #1—Confrontation is never easy. But confrontation without fortitude is never successful.

Good Failures

Failure is not always bad. In fact we learn more from our failures than we do from our successes. Abraham Lincoln's litany of failures is legendary. He failed in business and lost four elections before becoming the sixteenth President of the United States. R.H. Macy failed seven times before his store in New York caught on. Baseball legend Babe Ruth struck out 1,330 times. And Pulitzer Prize winner James Michener had been told by publishers, Hollywood producers, and

Broadway executives that his classic, *Tales of the South Pacific*, had no chance of being a hit.

It's not uncommon to witness, read, or hear about a person who publicly apologizes for his or her failures. What is uncommon is when the presentation becomes a "teachable" moment. Two examples follow:

Oops!

A number of years ago at a national convention, attendees were busy filing into the giant auditorium to hear a well-known speaker's presentation. The audience got settled just in time to hear the introduction. Many in the crowd anticipated that his keynote address would be the highlight of the conference. As the speaker walked to the podium, he motioned for the hotel's audio-visual expert to turn on the projector. Just as the lights were going down, the hotel employee started to reach for the "On" switch when suddenly he lost his balance and bumped the projector stand causing the carousel and all the slides to crash to the floor. The silence in the room was deafening. The speaker's face was bright red. And the hotel manager was rushing toward his employee to see how the embarrassing situation could be rectified.

At that moment the elderly gentleman who had caused the collision with the projector stand slowly walked up the center aisle from the back of the room passing more than two thousand conference attendees. Climbing on to the stage he approached the distraught keynote speaker and asked if he could address the audience.

Reaching for the microphone he said: "Ladies and Gentleman, I want to apologize for the delay in this morning's program. I have been doing this job for over thirty-five years and this is the first time I have ever messed up a speaker's slide presentation." He went on. "And if you can accept my apology and give me fifteen minutes, we'll get this show on the road." The audience jumped to their feet and gave this simple man a standing ovation.

In a similar display of humility a new CEO for an international company was addressing his worldwide leadership for the first time since joining the organization. After scanning his audience for a few seconds he began. "Ladies and gentlemen, I want to thank you for the rousing reception I received here this morning. And to give you a flavor for who I am and what I value, I want to share with you three of my failures."

The executive's first slide showed the picture of a new product with the word "FAILED" stamped diagonally over the image. "My program cost the company $20 million dollars." His second slide showed a picture of a manufacturing plant that again had a powerful one-word message written across the screen: "CLOSED." "It was my idea to open this operation before market intelligence could be confirmed." By now the audience couldn't wait for the finale. The last scene showed a line of men and women lining up for their unemployment check at a local government office. "Because of my blunder too many good men and women lost their jobs." The audience remained silent as their new boss turned off the projector. The CEO ended his presentation with these words: "Ladies and gentleman, if there is one message I want you to take away from this morning's presentation it is this: Failure is a good thing IF you learn from your mistakes. I have learned from mine. And now I look forward to working with others who are not afraid to take risks. Thank you for your valuable time." With that closing the new boss walked off the stage.

Fortitude Lesson #2—"Success is how high you bounce when you hit bottom."

General George S. Patton
World War II Commander 3rd Army

To Face the Wind

One of the best definitions of fortitude I've ever heard came from a parent in Phoenix, Arizona. I was visiting Jay and his wife Mary to learn why they were selected as one of the best parenting role models in the state. During my interview I asked Jay what he thought was the greatest gift he ever gave his children. He replied, "David, I've taught them *to face the wind.*" This father of two went on to explain that he knew that his son and daughter would sooner or later be called on to take a stand that demanded both courage and conviction. And "If I've done my job," he continued, "the kids will have the fortitude to face any situation."

Another set of nominated parents echoed Jay's sentiment. Colleen raised eight children with her husband, Terry, in Providence, Rhode Island. Daniel, the older child, told this story about his parents—one that illustrates the power of perseverance, a common trait associated with the gift of fortitude.

National Bunk Day is a time-honored tradition for high school seniors who supposedly earn the right to skip one day of school. For Daniel, this rite of passage was a given; or so he thought. Approaching his mother with confidence, he proudly announced he wasn't going to school the following day because all seniors were allowed to skip class. All Mom had to do was send a note with his younger brother stating that Daniel was ill. "You want me to do what?" his mother inquired. Her son began to argue that if his mom didn't sign the note that he would be the only high school senior going to class. "Your point?" she retorted. Daniel knew it was a hopeless case trying to convince either parent that he didn't have to attend school the next day.

That Friday morning Daniel got up, ate breakfast, grabbed his books, and went out the front door heading in the direction of the local high school. Later that evening the phone rang. It was Mr. Barrity, the high school principal, and he needed to speak to one of Daniel's parents. "Are you telling me that Daniel never showed up for class today?" an angry mother inquired. "Yes, Ma'ma, but today was National Bunk Day and none of our seniors came to school." The principal went on. "Mrs. Brown, all you have to do is tell me that your boy was sick and I'll approve an excused absence." "No, sir," came the emphatic response. "My son skipped school and I expect you will deal with his decision!"

It was a long weekend for Daniel as his "grounding" provided Mom and Dad plenty of opportunities to put their son to work. When Monday morning rolled around, Daniel did his best to get ready for school and the pending meeting with the principal. Few words were spoken between mother and son.

Daniel came home from school at the usual time. Going into the kitchen he found his mother preparing the evening meal. He walked up to her and said, "Mom, thank you." Somewhat suspicious, she looked her son straight in the eye and said, "For what?" Daniel continued, "After the principal told me I had detention for a week, he called a special meeting for all seniors in the auditorium." "And?" she inquired. "Well, Mom, Mr. Barrity reminded all the students and teachers in attendance that last Friday was National Bunk Day." "Oh yeah, I almost forgot about that stupid reason to skip school." Daniel's mom responded. "But listen, Mom, the principal said something else." "Go on." she countered. "Mr. Barrity said that the parents of over three hundred students sent notes to his office claiming that their son or daughter was sick. But here's the kicker, Mom. He looked right at me and said, 'Only one parent told the truth and her son should be proud of his mother.'"

Reflecting on this story I remembered a well-written series of inspirational messages by the United Technologies Corporation. Though they were published over twenty-five years ago, the series is timeless. One of my favorites follows:

Will The Real You Please Stand Up?

Submit to pressure from peers and you move down to their level. Speak up for your own beliefs and you invite them up to your level. If you move with the crowd you'll get no further than the crowd. When 40 million people believe in a dumb idea, it's still a dumb idea. Simply swimming with the tide leaves you nowhere. So if you believe in something that's good, honest, and bright—stand up for it. Maybe your peers will get smart and drift your way.

Fortitude Lesson #3 — "C" to the power of 3 — courage, conviction, and character—is the only theorem worth memorizing.

When There Is No Choice

Though fortitude offers additional strength to make a decision, there are times when a single course of action is the only choice. Three examples come to mind. First are those *Medal of Honor* winners who in a split second decided to save others by jumping on that grenade, running back to rescue the wounded, or staying behind to stall the enemy while other unit members could escape; a second example is Fr. Maximilian Kolbe, who took the place of a fellow Auschwitz prisoner that was scheduled to die in the starvation bunker. His unselfish action stunned Nazi camp guards who eventually put the priest to death. A third story revolves around a hospital "housekeeper" who inspired a very sick patient to fight the disease that had stricken her body. This cleaning lady offered one choice: never lose hope. The patient recovered and is especially grateful to the non-medical person who she believed was most responsible for a successful outcome.

The Golfer

Ronnie loved golf. After carding one "birdie" and two "pars" for a remarkable 46 the first nine holes he ever played, he was sure he had found his calling. I tried to explain something called, "beginner's luck," but my friend would have nothing of my reality. And to prove the point he immediately invited two others and me to join him for a second round of golf at a military base country club. We accepted.

After his poor tee shot on the first hole he found himself staring at a bridge that blocked his view of his second shot to the green. At the corner of the bridge was a skinny pole sticking up with a "sock" to warn golfers which way the wind was blowing. Ronnie took out his 5-wood and proceeded to hit a line drive right into the sock which promptly deposited his ball in the creek. His fellow golfers were quite impressed that anyone could somehow hit a size "six" sock from one hundred yards. At the end of the first hole, Ronnie was four over par.

As Ronnie teed up on the second hole, he found himself staring down a narrow shoot of trees. The last tree on the right before the fairway had a small can nailed to the trunk so golfers could deposit any trash they might have accumulated. Somehow the next "Tiger Woods" managed to hit an arching tee shot right into the red can which immediately vomited his ball out of bounds. Seven shots later, Ronnie was nine over par.

The next hole was a par three. After his tee shot our friend, who for some odd reason was strangely silent, found his ball only twenty yards away from the pin. However, he had to chip his ball over a sand trap that was guarding the green. He gently attempted to lift the ball over the trap. The only problem was the rake handle that somehow managed to deposit Ronnie's ball in the deepest part of the sand. Five shots later, "Lawrence of Arabia" emerged exhausted and covered in sand. A less than "perfect 10" was recorded.

By this time three golfers were checking their bags to see if anyone had any medication for uncontrollable laughter. Nothing was found.

Things settled down somewhat as Ronnie had navigated to within fifteen feet of the fourth green clear of the bunker that lay behind him. Looking around he said, "Well, I hit a sock, a garbage pail, and a rake handle. And as near as I can tell there is nothing between me and the pin." Apparently the "golf gods" were listening. As he struck the ball it appeared to be right on course. CLUNK! His ball had hit some mysterious object propelling it over Ronnie's head into the sand trap. With face flushed he charged the edge of the green to find out why his ball went backward. "I just hit a goddamn sprinkler head that failed to go back down," he screamed. At that moment our foursome became a threesome and three guys nearly wet themselves.

Fortitude Lesson #4—There are times when all the courage, conviction, and character in the world cannot change destiny.

Fortitude: The Fourth Principle for Great Leadership

General H. Norman Schwarzkopf was once quoted as saying, *"Leadership is a potent combination of strategy and character. But if you must be without one, be without the strategy."* The general could have said the same thing about courage and conviction. Collectively, these three attributes are what give a person the "fortitude" he or she needs to deal with personal pain and adversity. For those in leadership positions it comes with the territory.

“F” WORD FIVE

FORBEARANCE

"Endeavor to be always patient of the faults and imperfections of others for thou has many faults and imperfections of thine own that require forbearance."

—Thomas à Kempis
German Author of Devotional Literature

A number of years ago I came across a simple poem that was often attributed to Mother Teresa entitled, "Anyway." Originally written by Dr. Kent M. Keith when he published his Paradoxical Commandments in 1968, his words capture the essence of the seldom-used word—forbearance. For those who wish to lead, "Anyway" offers a roadmap that great leaders will ultimately experience.

"ANYWAY"

People are illogical, unreasonable, and self-centered. Love them anyway.
If you do good, people will accuse you of selfish ulterior motives. Do good anyway.
If you are successful, you will win false friends and true enemies. Succeed anyway.
The good you do today will be forgotten tomorrow. Do good anyway.
Honesty and frankness make you vulnerable. Be honest and frank anyway.
The biggest men and women with the biggest ideas can be shot down by the smallest men and women with the smallest minds. Think big anyway.
People favor underdogs but follow only top dogs. Fight for a few underdogs anyway.
What you spend years building may be destroyed overnight. Build anyway.
People really need help but may attack you if you do help them. Help people anyway.
Give the world the best you have and you'll get kicked in the teeth. Give the world the best you have anyway.

An obvious question is why anyone would continue to strive for goodness when they know that adversaries will never cease to criticize their actions, bad attitudes will always be present, and too many people believe they are entitled to that which they haven't earned. The answer is simple: success is measured by what one does for the greater good; failure, by what one does at the expense of others.

Reverse Resolve

Resiliency is a unique character trait that all great leaders possess. And as so often is the case, past experiences provide the best of life's lesson plans. In the following scenarios each main character had an experience that proved difficult to accept. But through the gift of forbearance they were all able to deal with a personal situation that made them stronger.

Scenario—1: Another name for progeria is the "aging disease." This rare congenital disorder affects children shortly after birth often taking their lives before they reach the age of twenty. It is a hideous affliction that causes children to lose their hair, teeth, and bone structure. Ten-year-olds look sixty years of age while teenagers resemble senior citizens in nursing homes. Asked to deliver a speech to parents whose children were living with this daily curse, I wondered what kind of message could possibly make a difference for those moms and dads whose "death watch" consumed them.

I arrived early and headed to the hotel conference room to listen in on a "teenage" discussion panel. There were three participants answering questions from an audience of grief-stricken parents. Scanning the forum, I couldn't differentiate whether a boy or girl was speaking. Even their voices were victims. One of the moms in the audience addressed a question to the teenager sitting in the middle of the group: "How do you cope with this terrible disease at a time in your life when you should be dating, going to the senior prom, and attending high school football games?" The response from this poor soul gave her sex away. "You know, I've got a choice," she said. "I can choose to complain about my life, or I can look at these handsome young men on my left and right and realize that they look just like me!" The girl's response got a thunderous ovation.

I searched for a logical explanation as to how this heart-breaking teenager could manage to laugh at her dreadful circumstances. Was there something in her genes that gave her the temperament needed to calm the sorrow that filled the room? Did her parents instruct her to put up a good front for the sake of younger progeria-stricken children in the audience? Or was it something else?

Scenario—2: Aunt Gerry was introduced to me through the memory of a gentleman named Steve Winegar. During our conversation he shared an amazing story about his favorite aunt. This lady contracted polio in the late 1930s. Aside from the hardship of caring for their daughter, her mom and dad had difficulty selling milk from the family farm because no one in the community understood how polio was transmitted. Gerry almost died and eventually ended up crippled her whole life. Nevertheless, she eventually married, had four children, was active in the community, and held leadership positions in many civic organizations.

Steve told me that at her 50th wedding anniversary, she was strapped in a motorized wheelchair and only able to be out of bed for one hour per day. She needed constant care and was attended to around the clock by her loving husband, Stuart. Gerry had endured dozens of operations and was suffering from post-polio syndrome when she died. Before she passed away, Steve asked his aunt what she would have changed in her life. Gerry thought for a moment, looked at her nephew and said,

"Nothing. My life's been perfect." What would drive a person like Gerry to have no regrets when her life of physical torment was license to complain?

Scenario—3: What happens when a ten-year-old girl is ridiculed by her parents for not catching the egg yoke on a single fork she was cleaning during her nightly dish-washing duty? And when these same parents continued their humiliation by sending their daughter to the store with a sign around her neck that read: "You are looking at someone who can't even clean the dishes." What kind of mother do you think she would turn out to be?

The answer became clear during my interview with a special mother and father who were nominated by a state teacher-of-the-year winner who participated in a national search for family excellence. During our conversation this remarkable woman shared the nightmare she faced growing up in a home where both parents did everything they could to destroy their daughter's self-worth. But somehow this child had the resiliency to overcome her childhood pain and become an outstanding role model for other women who one day would have children of their own. As the lady told me, "I resolved to never raise my children the way I was raised."

In all three examples the ability to accept difficult circumstances was manifested in both the action and attitude of the "victims." Clearly the gift of forbearance played a significant role as they faced unbearable conditions. This "reverse resolve" is a special talent that motivates the "afflicted" to accept the cards they have been dealt. And that trait often separates good from great leaders who recognize that the only guarantee in life, is that there are no guarantees.

Forbearance Lesson #1—"Compared to what?" Should be your first thought the next time you want to complain about your circumstances.

A Personal Journey

Over the years I have had to muster various "helpings" of forbearance. Reflecting back, I now realize that these personal trials and tribulations provided me with the "mettle" I needed to make tough decisions—a mandatory trait for those in leadership positions.

The Thief—I knew it would work. After all, how many families do you know have purchased five models of the same car for different reasons? Coming home from night school I noticed the different Vegas in the driveway of a home not far from where I lived. "Is it possible that one family actually purchased all five versions of Chevrolet's new Vega brand?" I thought. And if that were true, wouldn't someone from the corporation's advertising department want to use the family's story as a testimonial for their newest product offering?

Though I was only a blueprint operator working for one of the automaker's divisions, I knew which department to call to see if my idea had merit. Gathering my courage I dialed the office of Chevrolet's advertising director and asked to speak to the man in charge. After several attempts I finally reached the executive responsible for Vega advertising campaigns.

After I introduced myself, I began to explain I had stumbled on a home where five different Vegas were parked in the driveway. And should they all belong to the same family, wouldn't it make sense to create a campaign around the family's story showing the diversity of the product? After my pitch the gentleman on the other end of the line asked, "David, would you be willing to go to the home where you saw the cars and speak to the head of the household about your idea?" "You bet," I said.

The next evening I walked up to the house, rang the doorbell, and waited. A man in his early fifties answered the door. "Can I help you?" he asked. I briefly explained the reason for my visit. To my pleasant surprise he invited me to come inside and meet the other four Vega owners. Sure enough, five family members all drove different versions of the same car. Better yet, they all agreed to participate in a Chevrolet advertising campaign provided their dad's job as a General Motor's engineer didn't represent a conflict of interest. I was ecstatic.

The following day I called my Chevrolet "contact" to give him the good news. I knew that this was the break that would lead me away from paper cuts and foul-smelling pneumonia, into an exciting world of automotive advertising. I excitedly shared my conversation with the family and then asked the director what he saw as the next step. "Do you have the family's name and phone number?" he inquired. "Yes, sir," I responded. Seconds later he thanked me for the idea and hung up! That was it. No interest in my career. No offer to open doors. No job. I was devastated.

Five months later I saw a national commercial about a family in another state who had the same purchasing experience. I knew my idea had been hijacked. I also knew that I had to move on, get over my bitterness, and learn from the experience.

The Volunteer—"David," my boss began, "I want you to take over the volunteer department immediately." "Further," he continued, "the hospital auxiliary board is waiting to meet with you in conference room A." "Anything in particular I should be aware of, sir?" I inquired "One thing: your first call-to-action is to fire a volunteer." Stunned, I asked,

“Sir, how do you fire a volunteer?” His response was short and to the point. “Son, that is for you to figure out.”

Walking slowly to the conference room I contemplated my opening words to the hospital’s auxiliary leadership. Normally I would tell them about my background, mention how pleased I was to oversee the department, and elicit any recommendations that might make the organization stronger. But this situation was different.

After formal introductions I immediately brought up the issue about one of their members. “She’s got to go!” two of the ladies said simultaneously. “We should have taken this step last year,” another quipped. “Why didn’t you?” I inquired. All eyes drifted to the president. Her words stung my heart. “David, it’s not easy to release a volunteer who has served this institution for twenty years, averaging over twenty-five hours per week.” “But with that kind of dedication why on earth would you want to get rid of this person?” I asked in desperation. After listening to their complaints I had to admit that the individual in question had been demonstrating some bad, if not odd, behavior.

Three examples stood out. During her morning rounds outside of surgery she took it upon herself to express her condolences to a family whose loved one was already “under the knife.” The only problem was she decided to inform the anxious family that in her opinion the surgeon doing the cutting was incompetent! In a second case, the volunteer overheard one family member say to another, “Whatever happens is the will of God.” An avowed atheist, the hospital representative loudly retorted: “There is no God, so quit relying on someone that doesn’t exist.” Her last strike occurred after the auxiliary leadership transferred her to the gift shop, rationalizing that there was nothing she could do to embarrass the institution. Wrong! Days later, a young mother stopped in with two little children to purchase a gift for their grandma who was recovering from hip surgery. “Make sure your kids don't steal any candy," the childless volunteer yelled. That was the last straw.

Three days later I called a meeting with the auxiliary leadership and the volunteer who had given so much time to the hospital. As the defendant entered the room, she took one look at me and said, "You are here to fire me." And with those words the lady quietly exited the room.

The process was fair. The outcome was right. And the memory of that uncomfortable situation continues to fade. Still, relieving someone of her duties—someone who had given so much free time to the hospital—was extremely difficult.

The Demand—It was my second day on the job. I decided to meet my new staff and asked the department manager to set up one-on-one meetings with every person in the marketing division. The first individual I met was a fellow named George. After we shook hands, he sat down and immediately began to inform his manager's boss (that would be me) who in the department should be fired! I just listened as he ridiculed a fellow co-worker. Eventually I got around to other topics like: How long had he worked in the department? What were his main responsibilities? What did he think about the organization? Could he share something about his family, hobbies, or where he went to school? It seemed to me that these were the typical questions a staff member might expect the first time he meets the new vice president. But no, this guy was determined to convince me another fellow I had yet to interview was worthy of the axe! At the end of our conversation I thanked him for his time and said that I would take his advice under consideration.

Moments later, the gentleman I was supposed to fire walked in the room. And would you believe it, his opening salvo was to inform me that the best thing I could do for the division was to release my previous guest. Once again I remained silent choosing to listen to a second round of vitriolic commentary about another employee in the seven-person department!

The following morning I called the department secretary and said, "Martha, I want you to inform both George and Wayne that I want to see them in my office in fifteen minutes." I went on. "And Martha, have them drive over in one car." "Oh boy!" I heard her say as she hung up the phone. When my two disgruntled staff members entered my office, it was evident that both individuals were very uncomfortable in my presence. "Gentlemen," I began, "this is going to be a one-way conversation." I continued. "Yesterday I had the pleasure of meeting all my new staff. Unfortunately, it seems that both of you had a different agenda for the meeting." I paused to let my words sink in. "So here is some advice you may want to act upon." Their uneasiness was obvious. "One or both of you are going to learn how to work with each other; or, one or both of you will choose to leave the organization; or, I will end up firing one or both of you. The choice is yours. Have a nice day!"

I didn't want to begin my tenure by threatening some of my staff, but after they forced my hand I had little choice but to send a message that departmental infighting would not be tolerated. Two weeks later, Wayne resigned.

The Request—Barry and I were both professional colleagues and good friends. One evening my wife and I walked into our son's middle school gym to see Robbie and Barry's son, Michael, battle against cross-town rivals in a divisional basketball game. Just prior to the start of the contest Barry came over to where we were sitting and asked if I could speak with him privately. I excused myself from Cindy and followed Barry over to the far corner of the gym.

"David," he began. "I need to share something with you that is very disturbing and highly confidential." "What's up, Barry?" I asked. Lowering his voice he told me that another member on our executive team had been receiving sexual favors from certain members of the staff in return for administrative privileges. I was shocked. For over an hour we discussed how to address the situation with other organizational leadership. Satisfied that our plan was in place, we finished our conversation just as the boys' game ended. As I was walking over to my wife and victorious son, Barry asked me again to keep our conversation totally confidential until all parties were notified of the problem and appropriate steps were taken to rectify the situation.

His request was expected. However, I had one little problem. The gentleman in question was my neighbor, and MY DAUGHTER was his children's babysitter! I anticipated that Cindy would immediately inquire about the nature of my conversation with Michael's dad. The potentially explosive situation put me in a position with conflicting accountabilities. I had a responsibility to protect my fourteen-year-old daughter from any potential harm and an obligation to hold the sensitive information in confidence.

Cindy got right to the point. "What were you and Barry speaking about?" I took a deep breath and said, "Cindy, do you have faith in my decisions?" "Of course I do. What kind of remark is that?" she responded. I crafted my next words carefully. "Then I'm going to ask you to trust that there is a good reason why I can't answer your question." I went on. "But I promise that when the time is right you will be the first to know."

Later that evening I took my daughter aside and probed to see if there was any behavior my neighbor had displayed that I should be concerned about. Everything seemed in order. A short time later I felt comfortable sharing the information with Cindy. I was very relieved to hear her say that she was proud of how I protected both my daughter and my integrity.

If ever there was a time when I needed the strength to face difficult circumstances, that was it. And that strength had a name: forbearance.

Forbearance Lesson #2—There is good in every bad situation, and hope in every lost cause.

Helen's Hour

I've had the honor to work with some outstanding professionals, and as I mentioned in the chapter on *Fidelity*, one lady sticks out: Helen, the senior nursing executive who's wonderful leadership style helped her navigate her way down the hallways of a major Midwestern hospital.

As I was responsible for marketing, I frequently conducted focus groups with various customer segments to determine whether or not the patients and family members who used the hospital were satisfied with the service our nursing and physician staff rendered. After one particular session I learned that a number of mothers were livid with their pediatric emergency room experience. One story was particularly chilling.

A young mother brought her two-year-old child into the emergency room to get immediate care for his asthma. Sadly, this same little boy had spina bifida, a congenital defect in which the spinal column is imperfectly closed, often resulting in neurological disorders. As they were waiting in a cubicle to see the doctor, a new resident physician walked by. "Is that spina bifida?" he asked with morbid curiosity. "Yes," the boy's mother replied. The resident rushed to the child's side, picked him up, and pointed to the obvious deformity. "You know I've only seen pictures of this condition. Now I can say I've actually witnessed a real-life case." His callousness followed him out of the room. The mother was mortified. Her son was crying. And I had the video testimony needed to prove that this encounter actually happened in our pediatric emergency room.

As I shared the video with Helen, I could see her blood pressure rising as one story after another convicted her staff of failing to deliver a positive customer experience. Before the tape ended, Helen reached for the phone and dialed her assistant's number. "Janis, I want every one of my emergency room supervisors in my office in five minutes!" I was amazed that the receiver survived the crushing blow as it was slammed into its cradle. "David, would you please excuse yourself as I have to have a word with my staff."

Thirty-six hours later the emergency department customer service protocols had been revamped, the arrogant resident had been disciplined, and the relationship between the moms on the video and hospital personnel had been saved.

Forbearance Lesson #3—If your staff gives you reason to accept difficult circumstances or delay gratification, make sure they experience your compassion—a word which means "to suffer with."

Forbearance: It Goes With the Territory

High performing leaders seem to have that certain "grace" needed to face difficult circumstances. The following is representative of common trials and tribulations many outstanding CEO's have experienced during their climb up the ladder.

The Marketplace

- Government regulations and taxation restrain growth.
- Competition is fierce.

- Available talent to do the job is limited.
- Environmental disasters are unforeseen.

The Product or Service

- Raw materials are scarce.
- Quality is questionable.
- Service is non-existent.
- Research and development is lagging.
- Margins are too thin

The People

- A strong work ethic is the exception, not the rule.
- Unreasonable labor demands are self-serving.
- Recruitment and retention strategies are weak.
- Bad behavior by a few embarrasses the organization.

The Resources

- Capital dollars are limited.
- Time is short to meet investor demands.
- The energy to accomplish all that must be done is finite.

As daunting as the aforementioned list can be, the greatest challenge is the price leadership often demands in family relationships, one's health, and peace of mind. To diminish the impact these barriers have on professional and personal performance, great leaders draw their strength from a necessary attribute—forbearance. Their insight does two things: first, those who learn to accept difficult circumstances or delay gratification for a greater good, eventually learn how to balance obligations; second, complacency and bad decision making are significantly reduced in day-to-day encounters. Even so, there will be days when it seems the sky is falling regardless of one's title, span of control, or accountability. One "bad day" scenario follows:

- You wake up late, the car won't start, and your cell phone is at the office.
- When you finally arrive at work, you realize that you left the laundry at home, your son's game conflicts with an evening business meeting, and your assistant has called in sick again.
- The business day begins with a meeting with human resources to determine the plan-of-action for disciplining a supervisor whose personal problems have infected the entire office. At that meeting you learn that the background check on your number one candidate for a critical position has been "red-flagged."
- At the operations meeting the general manager reports that the corporate folks are again asking you to cut expenses to ensure that the quarterly financials look favorable to investors.
- After lunch your spouse calls asking if you can pick up your daughter at daycare. Your response isn't well received.
- Later that afternoon a key customer calls to inform you that unless the company improves its quality, she will be shifting business to your major competitor.
- As you are rushing out the door to attend the evening business meeting, your pager goes off signaling a problem with the new production line. Returning to the plant you realize that you will

> not only miss the dinner meeting but likely arrive too late to tuck your son and daughter into bed.

That night, you have trouble sleeping as you reflect on the past sixteen hours. In the silence of your bedroom you ask God to give you forbearance. As you drift off to sleep your last thoughts are gentle reminders that when it's all said and done, you are a very fortunate individual. For on this "bad" day, you did not get in a serious accident on your way to work; the doctor didn't call to say that the lab reports suggest a serious problem; your loving spouse "pinch-hit" for you during your son's game; the person you won't be hiring will also not be bringing their baggage to you; and though there are financial, staffing, and operational issues to address, you have an opportunity that tens-of-thousands can only dream about. All in all, you had a pretty good day.

"O Happy Days"

Recently I had the "week from hell." It started on a Monday with what I thought was going to be a routine checkup at the dentist. After the hygienist finished "raking" my teeth, Doctor Frankenstein entered the room. "So let's have a look," he began. "Oh dear," (two words you don't want to hear when sitting in that chair), "David, it looks like you need an immediate crown." Visions of pain and financial suffering danced in my head.

"Is it absolutely necessary to have this done this week?" I inquired. "I'm afraid so; otherwise, you might lose your entire tooth." The alternative was intriguing. "All right, let's get it done." I said. "Good decision," he responded. "I'll schedule your root canal for tomorrow." "ROOT CANAL? I thought I needed a gold crown," I objected. "You do," he said smiling, "but only after the endodontist gets through with you."

Tuesday's "digging," "probing," and "injections," were followed by Wednesday's crown construction, the latter which took four hours in the good dentist's chair. It was only after I returned home that I remembered I had a physical scheduled for Thursday which meant more "human suffering."

Thursday evening I returned home, poured myself a large glass of wine and planted my tortured body in the recliner. "Honey," my wife called out, "do not forget that your COLONSCOPY is scheduled at 7:00 a.m. tomorrow. So you can't drink any wine or have dinner."

At 4 a.m. Friday morning I sat on the pot waiting for the effects of thirty-two ounces of the most disgusting liquid imaginable to jump-start my system. After all, I wouldn't want "doctor rectum" to be inconvenienced. Half asleep, but fully aware, I too had to admit that I am a very fortunate human being. For at the end of the day (week), I was still on the right side of the sod!

Forbearance Lesson #4—There will be days when you will gladly choose a colonoscopy or root canal over your job.

Forbearance: The fifth principle for great leadership

The bumper sticker, "shit happens," the song "I Did It My Way," and the movie *The Good, The Bad, and The Ugly* all have something in common: each phrase could be the subtitle for a book on forbearance consisting of only two chapters and one simple prayer. Chapter one, entitled "It Is What It Is," says it all. And in case the reader didn't get the message, chapter two, entitled "Get Over It," would reinforce the point. The last page of the book on forbearance would end with a simple prayer often attributed to Saint Francis of Assisi.

> "*God grant me the **Serenity** to accept things*
> *I cannot change, **Courage** to change the things*
> *I can, and **Wisdom** to know the difference.*"

"F" WORD SIX

FORGIVENESS

> ***"The weak can never forgive. Forgiveness is the attribute of the strong."***
>
> ***—Mahatma Gandhi***
> ***Major Political and Spiritual Leader of India***

"Foot in Mouth" Disease

We've all done it. No sooner do the words leave our mouth and than the justification for our language, self-righteousness, and ego are manifested in the color on our face. It's especially embarrassing when our outburst was really intended to motivate another. Ask Jerry. He will tell you that all he intended to do was to encourage the young ballplayer to run faster so he wouldn't be thrown out by the shortstop. When he yelled, "Get the lead out," I couldn't help but notice how quickly the mother sitting in front of us turned around to glare at my colleague. "I'm sorry that my son doesn't meet your expectations, but that's probably because he has a physical deformity!" she responded. At that moment I denied any knowledge of ever knowing my life-long friend. Over the years I relished every opportunity to retell the story of a "coach" who failed to understand that it's a bit difficult to run to first base with braces on your legs.

You would think I would have learned from Jerry's faux pas, but no, I made an even bigger mistake. My son Robbie began organized sports after joining a local youth soccer team. During the first game I noticed that he wasn't hustling the way I thought he should. After all, like Jerry, I too knew something about coaching and motivating young children. "C'mon, Robbie, you can run faster than that," I shouted. "But, Daddy, I can't breathe," my nine-year-old responded. "Run! " I demanded. It was only when I saw his tears that I knew that something was holding him back. Two days later the doctor confirmed that Robbie had severe allergies. My impatience could have killed my child!

On another occasion I not only "put my foot in my mouth," but I also made a complete ass of myself in front of my boss who had every right to fire me for my behavior. The event happened when Les asked me to drive him to the airport, which was only five minutes from our corporate office. On the way to the terminal Les lit into me for what he believed was my failure to follow through on a project involving our advertising agency. I was livid! "Les, let me set you straight," I began. "The account executive who blames me for not communicating properly is the same person you accused of incompetence. Furthermore, if you would have taken the time to read my report, you would have discovered that the entire operating group has recommended that we change agency leadership." My tirade continued. "And since my performance has come into question, then I suggest that you either check your facts or fire me!" My last salvo ended just as I pulled the car up to the terminal. Les was silent; I was out of breath; and our parting was clearly strained.

As I drove away my anger gave pause to the reality that the man who was my mentor had silently walked away—something uncharacteristic of the person responsible for marketing an entire division of a *Fortune 500* company. A few minutes later, I was walking into my office when Cathy, our administrative assistant, came up and asked if she could have a private conversation with me. "What's up, Cathy?" I asked somewhat curtly. "David, I thought you ought to know that Les just called from the airport and he wanted me to tell you that you were right and he hopes you forgive him." My heart sank in an ocean of shame.

Who was I to rant at the man who had taken me under his wing when he could have hired a more experienced marketing manager? And did I forget that it was Les who insisted that I not return to work until Cindy and our newborn son were settled in their new home? And when it was all said and done, wasn't I responsible for accurate and timely communications between the marketing staff and outside agencies?

My conscience began to tear me apart. Though I had been insubordinate to my boss and deserved retribution for my behavior, I was more concerned that my words hurt the person I both trusted and deeply admired. It was a long five hours before I finally reached him. "Les, I'm the one who should apologize," I confessed. "David," he began, "all we did was have a little misunderstanding. That sometimes happens among team members. So let's forget it, move on, and continue to launch our marketing program." That day I was grateful that I worked for a man who understood the power of forgiveness. And to this day I do my best to remember what that single word can do for my soul and those I encounter in both my personal and professional life.

Forgiveness Lesson #1—Verbal recalls, like automotive recalls, are similar. Both pay a price to fix a problem that shouldn't have happened in the first place.

Kay's Way

One of the most powerful examples of forgiveness I have ever witnessed happened to a hospital volunteer. I received a call from the director of the department asking if I would be willing to sit down and listen to a lady who had a horrible experience in the emergency department. Such conversations were fairly common as I looked for opportunities to hear what our customers had to say about our services or set the record straight as to departmental protocols and staff accountabilities. But this encounter was so unbelievable that I asked Kay if she would be willing to repeat her story in front of a camera so that I could use her experience as a powerful teaching tool. Kay agreed, and with film rolling I proceeded to interview a hospital volunteer who had served the institution fourteen plus years while being a spokesperson for the organization in several promotional advertisements.

Kay had a severe cardiac condition. For fifteen years the local community hospital was the lifeline she needed as her transplant center was over two hours away. On several occasions her condition called for untimely visits to the local emergency room. On the night in question she desperately needed care as she awoke at 12:30 a.m. with pressure in her chest. When Kay and her husband arrived at the emergency center, there was no one present in the triage room. This experience was the beginning of a sixteen-hour nightmare. During her ordeal the hospital volunteer encountered one system breakdown after another, including the following:

- A triage nurse failed to properly check the sign-in log which resulted in further delays in Kay's initial treatment.
- Three staff members insisted that they could find the necessary vein to start an IV even after the patient warned the professionals that they should poke the vein in her hand instead of her arms. As a result, Kay was stuck no fewer than four times before a nurse finally realized that the patient's recommendation should have been followed.
- Two physicians neglected to advise the patient that she would have to be admitted.
- After Kay's husband went back home to get his wife's medicine, she called the front desk three times to get someone to help her go to the bathroom. Each time the patient was told, "We'll be right in." In desperation Kay rushed out of the cubicle to find the ladies room. She never made it. Kay urinated all over herself in a public area filled with hospital visitors.

- When a friend of the family took Kay to another area of the hospital to help her clean up, a supervisor chastised the patient by saying, "You need to return to the emergency room right now or your insurance is not going to pay for your visit!"
- After returning to the department, Kay was assigned to a different bed that was broken and unable to raise or lower her body to a more comfortable position. In addition, the call light didn't work. Kay had to sit straight up for over two hours. During this time she never received any food, water, or visit from a medical professional.
- She overheard one of the attending nurses ask, "So what's the status of the 'Prima Donna' in room twenty-seven?"
- A cardiologist said to Kay: "I understand that you are upset." And then followed with, "I couldn't care less about the problems you've experienced. My job is to treat your medical condition."

Ten minutes later the doctor agreed to sign the document releasing Kay from the hospital. Her ordeal had ended. When the interview was over, I asked Kay to sum up the experience. "Betrayed," was her one-word response.

Fortunately she agreed to allow me to share her story with hospital leadership hoping her message could be used to educate others on how not to treat a human being, especially one in dire need of medical care. Kay's message was so powerful that I opted to share our conversation at an executive management retreat where over 300 of the corporation's leaders sat in silence, shaking their heads in disbelief.

After the video ended, I walked up to the podium and said, "Ladies and gentlemen, what you just heard will hopefully energize your commitment to better customer service." Pausing for a moment, I continued. "And I know that everyone in this room would like to personally express how sorry they are that something like this happened to one of our patients." Again I hesitated for a few seconds to let my words take effect. "You will get that chance in a moment; but first Kay has a few words that may inspire your resolve to provide the best care your organization can deliver." I stopped, looked to the back of the room, and said, "Kay, would you please join me on stage?" As the video's star walked down the center aisle, I sensed a profound uneasiness in the room. After reaching the podium the retired teacher delivered a heartfelt commentary on why she agreed to address the audience. Her message was simple and to the point. "Sometimes a hospital family has its differences with the patients they serve. And unfortunately this volunteer got caught up in a situation that was uncomfortable for all of us." Kay continued. "But though I didn't receive the quality care that I have experienced in the past, I have decided that the healing process must begin." The room was still. "To that end," Kay continued, "I will be returning to my volunteer position at the hospital I dearly love!" Kay's two-minute address received a standing ovation. And to this day I have yet to witness a more humbling scene where the "victim," who had every right to condemn an audience, chose instead to take a higher road—forgiveness.

Forgiveness Lesson #2—"To err is human, to forgive divine."
Alexander Pope
Author and English Poet

A Simple Example

Few leaders have the opportunity to experience such dramatic encounters. But many will recall an episode where "forgiveness" set the tone for expected behavior. My lesson occurred at Children's Hospital Medical Center of Akron. As I was waiting outside the CEO's office for my weekly meeting, his door opened and out walked a director I didn't know very well. The individual exiting the boss's office was clearly upset.

"Come in, David," Bill said. I took my regular seat at his table situated in the corner of the room. Before I had a chance to go over my report, I heard my boss say, "I should just fire him!" I was surprised to hear these words from a leader whose personal and public reputation was beyond reproach … so much so, that everyone who worked for him had nothing but wonderful things to say about the person who became a CEO at age twenty-nine.

After listening to my boss discuss the reasons for his anger, I said, "Well, Bill, if you feel that way about the man's performance, why don't you just let him go?" Though my advice seemed logical, the words triggered a quick response. "David, my job is to inspire the best in my staff. And that means I still have work to do with this individual. If I give up on him now, it is I who failed." Bill's wisdom taught me that leadership demands that those in charge have the responsibility to go the extra mile when dealing with people. And over the years I have learned that "forgiveness" is the one asset that—when it comes to human capital—has the greatest return on investment.

Forgiveness Lesson #3—Know your place, lest you be replaced.

A Message From Dante

In the *Inferno*, the poet Dante and his guide Virgil travel to Hell by descending down nine circles of torment where one lost soul after another suffers. With each new encounter, Dante and Virgil witness greater and greater evil and their corresponding punishments.

Imagine a modern-day scenario where you are asked to visit nine unhappy souls who have offended you or embarrassed the organization.

Imagine further that their career is predicated on your willingness to forgive them. Could you: Forgive a colleague whose complacency left you holding the bag with your superior? Forgive the employee whose jokes make some in your department uncomfortable? Forgive the executive assistant whose attempt to protect your privacy alienates the customers? Forgive a manager whose thirst for recognition impedes departmental morale? Forgive the supervisor who brings his personal problems to work? Forgive the company "heretic" who talks out of two sides of his mouth? Forgive the senior executive who uses "intimidation" to get her point across? Forgive a co-worker whose behavior results in his personal gain at your personal loss? Forgive a friend whose relationship with a competitor puts you in a delicate situation with company management?

Those with leadership experience will argue that such "behaviors" should not be tolerated. True. However, it is one thing to take **serious** action against incompetent, immoral or insidious co-workers, staff, or senior leadership; it is quite another to condemn those whose operating, or management, "style" conflicts with how you believe people should conduct themselves.

To begin the "healing" process great leaders will exhaust every option available hoping to rebuild a relationship with the person whose actions must be addressed. But even if initial steps are successful, the power to both "forgive and forget" is extremely difficult; or as the humorist Kin Hubbard wrote: "*Nobody forgets where they buried the hatchet.*"

The Father I Never Knew

A very personal experience looks at "forgiveness" from a different perspective. My mother was born in Scotland and met my father after WWII in Germany. He convinced her to leave her family and move to the United States; hence, I was born in Black River Falls, Wisconsin, instead of Clydebank, Scotland. Unfortunately, my mom and dad were divorced when I was only six months old. My mother not only chose to remain in America (moving to Michigan), but she also chose to never remarry. As a result I grew up with no father, brothers, sisters, aunts, uncles, or grandparents. Nevertheless, I had a happy childhood even though I never heard my father's voice, received a letter from him, or had a photograph of the man responsible for my existence.

This all changed one Saturday morning as I was preparing to leave for baseball practice. Suddenly the phone rang. Pausing for a moment, I waited to see if the call was for me. After speaking briefly with the caller my mother handed me the phone and said, "Your father is on the line." Stunned, I hesitated for a few seconds and then took the receiver from my mother. "Hello." "This is your father," was the reply. His words nearly knocked the wind out of me. My poor attempt to get the "D" word out was evident to the man on the other end of the line. "Son," he continued, "I wanted to get in touch with you to let you know that I think of you quite often." I remained silent. "Perhaps you could drop me a line or give me a call sometime," he pleaded. By this time my mother had walked into the other room to give her sixteen-year-old boy some privacy with his dad. "I guess I could do that," I stammered. After a few more minutes of one-way conversation we hung up. My mother never asked what her ex-husband said. It didn't matter much anyways, as I wouldn't speak to him for another seven years.

A few days after my marriage to my wife, Cindy, we received a wedding gift from my father. It dawned on me that my mother called my grandmother (whom I never met) and informed her that her grandson had just taken a new bride. I now had no choice but to pick up the phone and thank the man who was reaching out to me. From that moment on we exchanged phone "pleasantries" on Father's Day and Christmas.

Four years later my father invited Cindy and me to Wisconsin to celebrate Thanksgiving Day with his family. Though I was unprepared for this second request, I was more mature and immediately accepted his invitation. Two days before we left I received a different message. Mary, who I learned was my half-sister, called to inform Cindy and me that the invitation was off because my father was too nervous to meet the son he never raised.

Nine years later Mary called again. "David, I know you are disappointed with past events, but the time is now right for a father and son to get together." She went on to explain that my dad's health was poor and that he was hoping to meet his first-born child before he died. "And just how should we arrange this meeting?" I asked sarcastically. "David, you have to take the initiative and fly up to Wisconsin. But it's important that you don't tell him you are coming because he won't be able to handle the stress." Oh sure, I thought, I'll just walk up to his door, ring the bell, and when he answers, I'll say, "Hi, Dad, how have you been these past thirty-six years?" I finished my conversation with Mary promising to give her latest invitation some consideration.

A month later I decided to call my dad and leave him a message announcing the time my plane would be arriving in La Crosse, Wisconsin. I had no idea whether he would show up at the airport. When I got off the plane I went to the baggage area, collected my belongings and waited. For a moment I thought I was the only person in the terminal. Suddenly my eye caught the image of a stocky gentleman dressed in overalls and wearing a big farmer's hat. "NO," I thought, surely he wasn't my dad. Slowly the stranger came up to the unclaimed visitor. "You must be my father," I stated. "And you must be my son," he responded; thus began a twenty-four-hour visit to catch up on almost four decades of lost conversations.

It would have been very easy for me to criticize my dad for waiting so long before he reached out to his son. But who was I to question what he did or failed to do? For whatever reason, I grew up in a single-parent home. I never wanted for anything, I never got into trouble, and somehow I managed to turn out ok. For these reasons, it was not my place to demand that my father ask forgiveness. On the contrary, it was my responsibility to share a memory of my dad with his grandchildren. In the end, how could I condemn a man I never knew?

Something to Ponder

I share this story as a reminder that there will be situations where another's actions deserve immediate retribution. But there will also be times when bad behavior is triggered by something we don't understand. Family pressures, internal illness, loss of loved ones, financial stress, and a host of other issues, both internal and external, may be the direct cause for one person or another acting out. For those who wish to lead, reconciliation can unlock the "whys" of poor performance and attitude.

Hopefully these words will resonate as you reflect over the wrongs of your own past life. Do you recall a situation when you acted as judge and jury, poisoned others with your comments or actions, lost control in your anger, complained about everyone and everything, acted with personal self-interest, or were suspicious of others' good fortune? Were not these the times when you needed forgiveness? And when you received that gift, did you not breathe a sigh of relief knowing you had a second chance? Wasn't a weight lifted off your shoulders? Wasn't your conscience cleared?

I'm sure everyone has heard stories of individuals whose ability to forgive the wrongdoing of others is astonishing. The best example I ever came across happened in Italy at the turn of the century. Maria Goretti was not yet a teenager when a nineteen-year-old man named Alessandro approached the young girl for sexual favors. As she fought off her attacker, he pulled out a knife and stabbed the virgin fourteen times. As the young girl lay dying, Maria told a priest that she had forgiven the assailant who had caused her so much suffering. Twenty-seven years later, Alessandro was released from prison. Shortly thereafter he arranged a meeting with his victim's mother to ask for forgiveness for what he had done. Mrs. Goretti replied, "Maria has forgiven you. Must I also not forgive you?" This ultimate act of reconciliation occurred on Christmas Eve. Hours later, mother and murderer attended the Vigil Mass.

Remember Gandhi's words: "*The weak can never forgive. Forgiveness is the attribute of the strong.*" Although Alessandro overpowered the girl, she clearly demonstrated greater strength through her absolution than he did through his attack. Forgiveness is not easy. It requires great strength of character and will power. Some might call this trait a sign of weakness; others recognize the power of forgiveness for what it is—an opportunity to salvage a relationship. But the choice is yours. You can condemn, or forgive. But if you want a good night's sleep, I would recommend the latter.

Forgiveness Lesson #4—"Forgiveness is not an occasional act. It is a permanent attitude."

Martin Luther King, Jr.
American Civil Rights Leader

Forgiveness: The Sixth Principle for Great Leadership

In the twelfth century, a Jewish theologian and physician by the name of Maimonides wrote about the ways we can choose to help others. His commentary on charity became known as ***The Chamber of the Silent.***

With each new level there is a greater call to humility. As I studied the author's degrees of kindness, I couldn't help but think that his separations also apply to forgiveness. So with apologies to the good doctor, allow me to propose seven degrees of pardon that may well define the difference between bad, good, and great leadership.

- The first degree: To forgive with reluctance or regret.
- The second degree: To forgive, but not proportionately to the offense committed.
- The third degree: To forgive proportionately, but not until the other person begs for mercy.
- The fourth degree: To forgive, but in so doing eliciting unnecessary shame.
- The fifth degree: To forgive in a way that brings adulation to you.
- The sixth degree: To forgive in a way that keeps the matter between you and the forgiven private.
- The seventh degree: To forgive in secrecy, choosing to move beyond the issue.

If you find the sixth and seventh degree difficult to accept, then I suggest you memorize Matthew 6:14, where Jesus said to his apostles: ***"If you forgive others their transgressions, your heavenly Father will forgive you. But if you do not forgive others, neither will your Father forgive your transgressions."***

"F" WORD SEVEN

FAITH

> ***"Faith is believing in things when common sense tells you not to."***
>
> ***—George Seaton***
> ***American Playwright who won an Oscar for the movie, Miracle On 34 th Street***

Eureka

Regardless what the studies show, consultants present, or common sense demands, there will be times when leadership calls for a higher analysis—one that can't be proven until the decision is made and executed. Some call it a "hunch." I prefer "faith." My daring can be attributed to the woman I married.

The bowling scoreboard identified the pretty blonde as Cindy. With that knowledge and a little courage, I got the nerve up to ask where she lived. "I can't see boys," was her answer. Undeterred, I tried another approach. "What's your last name?" Again, her response was the same. "I understand," I said; "I was just curious." Recognizing my intentions, Cindy coyly said, "Detroit." "Huh?" "Detroit, that's where I live," she teased. My future search had just been narrowed down to a city of over 1 million people. I figured that with some gentle persuasion, more detailed information might be forthcoming. I made a third inquiry. "What part of Detroit?" I asked. With a half smile she said, "Well, I live on a street, near a street, named Eureka." With this new intelligence I figured I better not press my luck.

The following day, July 9, 1964, at approximately one in the afternoon, my friend Randy stopped by. I immediately tried to convince him to help me find the blue-eyed blonde I had met the day before. "Let me see if I've got this right," he said. "You met this girl named Cindy, who wouldn't give you her last name, phone number, or address, other than the fact that she lives 'on a street, near a street, named Eureka.'" "You got it," I responded. "Furthermore," Randy continued, "according to your map, Eureka runs SIX MILES!" "Correct," I confirmed. "Are you nuts?" he demanded to know. "C'mon, Randy, we've got nothing to do anyways. Let's just walk into Detroit and see if we can find her." I added, "Besides, you've got to have faith in these matters." After five minutes of debate, Randy finally agreed to join in the search for a girl that, as he said, "may not even be home, wherever that is."

We followed the map toward the mythical land of Eureka. Running out of conversation, Randy finally stopped. "Look, David," he began, we have been walking for almost an hour in ninety-degree heat and we still don't know if we have one or five miles to go." His logic was hard to refute. "Randy, we can't stop now. Eureka is the next street." "True," came his terse reply, "however, you do recall that she said she doesn't live on Eureka!" I resigned and we turned down Justine Avenue to head back home. As we walked in silence, I noticed a little girl about six years of age heading toward us. For some strange reason I flagged her down. "By any chance, do you know of any girl named Cindy that lives around here?" I inquired. Without hesitating, the child pointed to the house we were standing in front of and said, "Cindy lives right there." The girl I was looking for was sitting in the backyard with her sister, Nancy. It was her birthday. And as of this writing, Cindy and I have been married for thirty-eight years! Postscript: *Eureka*, is the Greek word for "I have found."

The Sign

A number of years later I had the pleasure of speaking to a very successful executive who had experienced his own "Eureka." As one of the top salesmen in his company, Jeremy was offered the opportunity to start a new division in the educational field. After accepting the assignment he immediately began marketing the program to school superintendents.

He made sales calls. He attended trade shows. He advertised his services in educational journals. For months he tried every technique possible but failed to land a single lead, much less a client.

As depression began to set in, he decided that it was in his best interest and the interest of the organization to shut down the program. On a Thursday Jeremy called his secretary and asked her to make an appointment with the CEO for the following week. That evening he received a phone call from a friend who suggested that he attend a dinner function on Saturday where superintendents and other education leadership would be in attendance. "Who knows," his friend opined, "you may meet someone who will help you break into the business." Reluctantly, Jeremy agreed to attend.

The weather was terrible that evening, and the forecast was calling for an additional six inches of snow. After parking his car he crossed the street and headed straight for the convention hall. Suddenly he was startled to see a stranger standing in the middle of the road in spite of the blizzard conditions. As Jeremy later stated, "I don't understand how I didn't notice him. It was almost as if he came out of nowhere." The man standing in front of Jeremy said nothing, only offering his hand. Jeremy told me that he rarely gave money to "street" people. But for some reason he stopped, took out his wallet, and handed the stranger five dollars. The intruder nodded his approval and without saying anything he handed what Jeremy thought was a business card. He discovered that the stranger's gift only listed sign language symbols used by people who were deaf and couldn't speak. Sticking the card in his shirt pocket Jeremy proceeded to the convention hall.

For the umpteenth time the outcome was the same. Not a single person was interested in either Jeremy's services or Jeremy himself. He left the meeting a broken man. Later that evening in the privacy of his apartment, he broke down and cried out to God. "Lord, I've failed.

And come Monday I'm going to admit my failure. But if this is a business I can serve you in, I need a sign."

That Monday morning, Jeremy was heading directly to the CEO's office when his secretary intercepted him in the hallway to show her boss a Sunday newspaper from a large East Coast city. Simultaneously another manager, who had just returned from the West Coast, came up to Jeremy and handed him a newspaper from a major city in California. Both the secretary and the manager had circled an advertisement in the business ad section. Jeremy looked at both papers, smiled, turned to his secretary, and said, "Martha, cancel my appointment with the CEO. There is business waiting for us." I asked Jeremy how he knew. "David, he said, "both advertisements were asking suppliers to submit a 'request for proposal' in the very service line I was desperately trying to sell." "But Jeremy," I interrupted, "how did you know that this was the sign you asked for?" Jeremy smiled. "David, both ads were sponsored by schools for the deaf!"

Katrina

The images told the story. Mothers and fathers clinging to their children as they boarded busses to some unknown destination, elderly residents wandering flooded streets, stranded pets seeking dry land, police officers trying to enforce law and order, firemen desperately trying to stop entire neighborhoods from burning down, volunteers going house to house searching for hurricane victims, hospital personnel struggling to keep their patients alive, scenes of destruction courtesy of massive television and magazine coverage, and unbelievable sorrow in the faces of tens of thousands as they struggled to survive America's worst natural disaster.

Many citizens blamed local and national authorities for reacting too slowly. Some politicians pointed fingers at the opposing party implying that had they been in power, things would have been different. And too many media personalities sat in the comfort of their national television studios conducting numerous "witch hunts." Some of their targets were police officers who abandoned their duty to see if their own families were alive.

Disease, death, and despair riddled the nation's heart. But something else caught our attention. The sight of joy on the faces of first responders who rescued children from certain drowning gave us hope. Volunteers from all over the country feeding homeless victims, animals, and exhausted police, military, and firemen, gave us a sense of pride. And thousands of national, state, and local organizations that led a "call to action" gave all of us the opportunity to serve others.

Like most Americans, I was glued to the television set waiting for the nightly news to send more images of human suffering. Daily newspapers supported the visuals with a blow-by-blow description of the tragedy. And talk show hosts added their "two-cents" worth of commentary designed to guarantee their network's ratings. Yet nothing impacted me more than a series of emails written by a military officer who described the horror facing the people of New Orleans. From floating bodies to shipwrecked vessels, from garbage to stench, from human cesspools to human suffering, this soldier saw it all.

But he saw something else. While wading into a chapel, his attention was drawn to a painting that hung above the altar. It was a picture of a man hanging on to a wooden cross in the middle of a raging sea. For this officer, the image was a powerful reminder that in times of peril, our only hope rests with the faith one has in God.

Faith Lesson #1—"ADD"—adversity, doubt, despair—has only one prescription: faith.

Vision

Business plans address it. College professors teach it. Consultants draft it. And great leaders live it. "It" is vision. For without the ability to articulate your dream you run the risk of failure; at least that's what the experts will tell you. But there are those individuals whose "vision" came to light almost by accident. Three examples come to mind.

In the chapter on *Fortitude*, I introduced Colleen Brown, the mother who taught her son that "National Bunk Day" was no excuse for not going to school. This was the same lady who disagreed with her father and chose to marry a man he didn't feel was right for his daughter. The reason: Colleen was in love with a blind man. "What do you see in this man?" her dad demanded to know. "It's quite simple, Dad," Colleen responded. "I know he will be both an outstanding husband to me and provider for our family." And to prove the point, Colleen and her husband, Terry, had eight beautiful children; and Terry was honored as the "Handicapped Person of the Year" for his contributions in both his personal and professional life. One can only wonder if he would have accomplished as much were it not for the "vision" Colleen had for the kind of man she wanted to marry.

Geoff Gursel had a different kind of "vision" experience. At age twenty-two this handsome, engaging, intelligent young man chose to give back before taking what the world might offer him. He joined the Peace Corps and ended up in one of the poorest countries on earth, Gabon, Africa. For over two years Geoff had the responsibility to teach African children how to speak English. But for this teacher, his class would be unlike any in America. There were seventy-five students: over half had malaria, five had AIDS, and six girls under the age of fifteen were pregnant. Coughing jacks, broken crutches, and labor pains competed with daily lesson plans.

During his tenure with the Peace Corps, Geoff wrote several letters to family and friends. In one letter he said, "Letting 'my children' go wild with magic markers and crayons, let alone plain paper which they've never seen, makes both me and them smile." He went on. "I see the malnourished children, stomachs way too wide, literally starving for food. I see our filthiness. I see our bamboo shacks. But then I notice something. Amidst all that poverty I hear laughter. I 'hear' smiling." Geoff continued. "I see people suffering. I see them starving. But then I see them differently. The simplicity of their happiness is nothing short of astounding!"

In the same correspondence Geoff pointed out how "human touch" transcends any donation, political vote, or good-will package. And with this reality he had the courage to admit: "Something is making these people find joy in something we would find joyless. And though it's tough to have faith among such sorrow I now understand that God sometimes hides his answers." The Peace Corps volunteer ended with this thought: "He hides them in little villages days into the Central African jungle. And it is up to us to find them, no matter how hard that might be. Fortunately for me, I see God in a little girl's laughter."

Colleen had a "vision" of what could be. Geoff's vision was of what is. But for John Shinsky, his vision was driven by the belief that God would open several doors allowing him to build a children's orphanage. That faith began to materialize during a business trip to Texas where on a plane he sat next to a young man who was working at an orphanage during spring break. This chance encounter resulted in John's visit to a special home for poor children, which eventually led to a meeting with two sisters, ages 92 and 100, who challenged John to pursue his dream to build The City of Children.

But as the Epistle of James 2:26 reads: "*Faith without works is dead.*" That's why John began placing calls to a few key friends. First there was a CEO of a busing company who agreed to provide the necessary transportation of labor and materials to Matamoros, Mexico. Then a retired professional athlete, whose bronze image now sits in the Football Hall of Fame in Canton, Ohio, agreed to contact other ex-professional players to ask for their help in raising money. There was the attorney who offered to handle all legal documents; the chief financial officer and international consultant who opened the door to Rotarian members made up of numerous business leadership; and most of all, John's devoted wife and partner, Cindy, without whose support John's dream would have been all but impossible.

When I learned of John's project, I had to ask why he believed such a city could be built. "David," he replied, "who would have thought that I, a past orphan, would have been in a position to one day build an orphanage? And could anyone have predicted that this academic all-American football player would give up a chance to play in the NFL for an opportunity to help children?" John continued. "And could I have imagined that two elderly sisters would have helped me understand what's important in life? Or that I would attempt to build my orphanage in a place where I can't even speak the language?" John's last comment crystallized his vision. "Besides, David, God has been behind me from the beginning. He has come too far to back out now!"

Colleen, Geoff, and John have three things in common. First, each accepted a challenge that few have the conviction or heart to undertake. Second, all three individuals had a "vision" that what they chose to do was the right decision. And third, their faith in God's divine plan gave them the courage to persevere in love and service to others.

Faith Lesson #2—Conviction, vision, and faith represent three tenets of successful leadership. And the greatest of these is faith.

Be Not Afraid

"Leadership" has several definitions including "one that leads or guides; one in charge or in command of others; one who has power or influence." The example *Webster's New College Dictionary* provides refers to the conductor of an orchestra. I found this analogy particularly prophetic given a comment by Max Lucado. The inspirational author is quoted as saying, *"A man who wants to lead the orchestra must turn his back on the crowd."* Those who are chosen to lead must sometimes make decisions that do not sit well with certain staff, decision makers, customers, board members or investment analysts. Nevertheless, great leaders don't achieve great results by genuflecting to other agendas. They are successful because they have the "guts" to do what they believe is right and the "faith" necessary to get them through their darkest hours. Examples of "greatness" follow:

During the American Revolutionary War a British officer got separated from his unit. Realizing that the Continental Army was nearby, he carefully moved through the forest hoping to remain undetected. The officer came to a small clearing where he saw another military leader on his knees with his head bowed. Moving closer he realized that the man praying was wearing a Continental Army uniform. He silently listened to his prayers. Sometime later, the British officer found his way back to his unit and headed straight for his tent. He pulled out his diary and made the following notation: *"When I saw the sight, I knew we were defeated. For any army whose commander was so humble before almighty God could never lose the war."* The commander the officer was referring to was General George Washington!

In the early years of WWII the newly elected Prime Minister of Great Britain, Winston Churchill, gave a stirring speech before the House of Commons. His words will never be forgotten.

> "You ask what is our aim? I can answer in one word: It is Victory, victory at all costs, victory in spite of all terror, victory, however long and hard the road may be; for without victory, there is no survival ... We shall fight on the beaches, we shall fight on the landing grounds, we shall fight in the fields and in the streets, we shall fight in the hills; we shall never surrender. Let us therefore brace ourselves to our duty, and so bear ourselves that, if the British Commonwealth lasts for a thousand years, men will say, 'This was their finest hour.'"

Though the Nazi war machine had superior numbers, the British Royal Air Force fought gallantly, eventually forcing the German high command to abandon their land and sea invasion. During this fight for survival Churchill had little patience for British leaders who dwelled on past failures. To them the Prime Minister warned, "*Of this I am quite sure, that if we open a quarrel between the past and the present, we shall find that we have lost the future.*"

For Helen Keller, the odds of living a normal life were astronomical. At eighteen months of age she was stricken with an illness that made her deaf, blind, and unable to speak. Five years later twenty-year-old Anne Sullivan was hired to teach the little girl how to communicate. Sullivan's daunting task was captured in the movie *The Miracle Worker,* starring Anne Bancroft as Anne Sullivan and Patty Duke as Helen Keller. Teacher and student were both successful. Annie Sullivan's student finally learned to communicate. And as for Helen, her achievements would startle audiences around the world as the person who was deaf, dumb, and blind, entered Radcliffe College graduating cum laude with honors in German and English; learned to speak Greek; wrote her autobiography, *The Story of My Life;* and received the Presidential Medal of Freedom. In later years Helen Keller said, *"I believe that all through these dark and silent years, God has been using my life for a purpose I do not know. But one day I shall understand and then I will be satisfied."*

Another successful teacher-student encounter was captured in the book *Seabiscuit: An American Legend.* The story of the famous horse that defeated the invincible War Admiral—the most successful racehorse of the day—became a symbol of hope for many who struggled during the Great Depression. Both trainer Tom Smith and jockey Red Pollard were responsible for leading the undersized, knobby-kneed animal to greatness. In 2003 the story of Seabiscuit was made into a movie that received a nomination for an Academy Award for Best Picture.

"Be not afraid" were the first three words uttered by Pope John Paul II in 1978 as he began his pontificate as head of one billion Catholics. And during his life this Polish son defied the Soviet empire, Western culture, Church hierarchy, and an assassin's attempt on his life. He proceeded to do what he believed was best for the people he served. When he died his funeral was the single most watched and downloaded event in the history of the world. Interestingly, the man Pope John Paul II admired most used the same three words to comfort a handful of friends over two thousand years earlier.

Faith Lesson #3—History is filled with great leaders who refused to believe there is no hope, there is no chance, there is no God.

The Assessment

I recently reviewed a document that provided information on the leadership style of a candidate who was seeking an executive position. The psychological profile offered critical insights on the applicant including problem solving skills, motivation, interpersonal characteristics, and overall personal adjustment. I have provided specific commentary from the report. I have also taken the liberty to pose five questions that I believe the analysis fails to address.

Leadership Style—The candidate possesses an operationally orientated leadership style. He is focused on practical results and is relatively tactical in his orientation. He plans effectively and follows through to see that goals are accomplished. He is structured, systematic, and detail-orientated. He is socially engaged and takes an intuitive and empathic approach to managing people. He is likely to work particularly well with people in a one-to-one mentoring relationship.

But how will the candidate handle failure?

Problem Solving—The candidate is focused, disciplined, and systematic in his analytical and decision-making approach. He is more conservative than risk-orientated. He does have a tender-minded side and to some degree will allow his feelings for people to influence his judgments.

But can he manage the "unexpected"?

Motivation—The candidate is solidly motivated and takes his responsibilities seriously. He can be of assistance to people, and he enjoys the accountability for helping them achieve their goals. As a result, he balances his drive with interpersonal sensitivity.

But what impact will personal pressures have on his performance?

Interpersonal Characteristics—The candidate enjoys working with people but can work independently as well. He is a highly empathic individual who is particularly sensitive to the needs of others. He is team-orientated, collaborative, and facilitative in his interpersonal management style.

But how will the candidate deal with professional betrayal?

Personal Adjustment—The candidate is an emotionally calm, steady, and well-adjusted individual. He has good tolerance for stress and pressure. He is typically patient and tolerant in his dealings with people. He maintains a positive and optimistic outlook even when faced with difficulties and adversity.

But where does he turn when everyone turns against him?

Psychological testing, past work history, reference checks, background investigations, and personal interviews represent the hiring menu used to select ideal candidates for leadership positions. All this is good. But I believe the best solution for handling failure, the unexpected, pressure, betrayal, and abandonment is faith in God.

Faith: The Seventh Principle for Great Leadership

The seven principles for great leadership are all critically important. But for me, the most important attribute is "faith." For without a spiritual foundation those who are called to lead have little or nothing to fall back on when personal crisis occurs, the professional environment crumbles, or the physical condition deteriorates. Leaders and non-leaders alike typically summon family and friends to help weather the storm. And many of these same individuals do reach out to God when stress and despair begin to take their toll. But for many great leaders—whether CEO's or supervisors, superintendents or kindergarten teachers, major league managers or youth baseball coaches, generals or sergeants—trust in God is the "bottom line" long before the hour of trial and tribulation begins. And when that hour does come—as it most certainly will—the strength to face adversity will be there.

A FINAL STORY

Some believe that certain individuals were born to be great leaders. Others suggest that great leadership develops over time. For my money, I believe that every person is "wired" in a different way. I also believe that these "differences" have a direct impact on how we are both seen and judged by others. For some people "leadership" is a calling. For others, it is an accountability driven by one's job description, position in the family, and/or reputation in the community. There are those individuals who are blessed with the opportunity to lead and inspire many. And there are people who simply make a profound difference in one person's life.

Regardless, the road we follow often has nothing to do with our personal desires and everything to do with the Will of God. One minute you are quite content with your progress, and the next moment someone invades your space to offer different options. I learned this lesson over thirty years ago.

I was attending night classes for my graduate degree at Wayne State University in downtown Detroit. One evening just days before Christmas, I decided to visit a little church located on the corner of the main campus. A prayer or two before final exams seemed an appropriate pre-test strategy for someone who never tested well. Because it was the dinner hour, the chapel was empty. After settling down for a private reflection, I sensed someone looking at me. Turning around, I was startled to see a young man some twenty feet away just staring at me. Feeling uneasy I asked, "Is there anything I can help you with?" The stranger responded, "Perhaps you can. I just drove into town with my wife and newborn son and we don't have any place to stay." Recognizing a scam in progress, I asked, "And just where is your wife and son?" "They are in the car outside in front of the church," he responded. I didn't believe his story and didn't trust his intentions.

"Listen," I said, "go next door to the rectory and the parish priest will help you and your family." The stranger politely nodded and seemed grateful for my suggestion. I turned back to face the altar. But because I was unsettled by his presence, I immediately looked over my shoulder to make sure the intruder was leaving. The only problem was he was GONE! Jumping up from my seat, I quickly checked all the pews nearby to see where he was hiding. He wasn't to be found. I ran outside. There was no car, no wife, no baby, and no stranger. My visitor had vanished.

I rushed off to class replaying the encounter in my mind. That evening, I could barely concentrate on the exam questions. Before the session ended, I said this silent prayer: "Lord, I don't know what I experienced tonight. But if that was You in any way, please give me a sign." When class ended six of us proceeded to the parking garage. I offered little conversation as my conscience continued to trouble me. Approaching a cross street, we noticed a homeless man sitting on the curb. He was shivering with cold. Just before I passed him he stood up, stepped in front of me, and said, "Could you spare some change for a warm cup of coffee? But you don't have to touch my unclean hands, just throw your coins in the gutter." I was shaking as I reached for my wallet, hoping I had enough cash to settle my spiritual debt.

Over the years, I have shared that story with audiences from all walks of life. My message is always the same: You never know who will come into your life and touch you in such a way that you now have the accountability to touch others.

Thirty years after that bone-chilling experience, the memory of that evening hit home once again. At a fundraising dinner I was approached by a well-known community attorney. "David," he began, "you don't know what impact you have had on me." Puzzled, I responded, "Jim, I'm not sure I understand what you are saying." He smiled and said, "I was in the audience during one of your presentations when you told that story about the stranger in the chapel. The following day I was standing in line at a grocery store with five other patrons. Suddenly a woman approached the six of us. In desperation she cried out, 'Can someone please help me?'" Jim went on, "David, she appeared to be drunk slurring her words and acting strange. One fellow standing next to me remarked, 'Maybe if we all chip in and buy her a bottle of booze we can solve her problems.'" I began to sense where Jim was heading as he continued his story. "Though I felt uncomfortable with the remark, I hesitated to step forward and offer assistance. It was then that I recalled what happened to you that night in the chapel." Jim took a deep breath. "I left the line, walked up to the struggling woman, and said, 'How can I help you?' 'Sir,' the lady weakly responded, 'could you please get me some orange juice?'" Jim knew I failed to grasp his point. "David, the moment she said those words I realized that the woman was having a diabetic attack and had I not stopped to help her, she could have died!"

I don't know how many other "Jims" have heard about my encounter with the stranger in the chapel, nor will I ever know how many people have been impacted by what I've done or failed to do. But I do believe that if I use whatever talents I have for the greater good, then the same Power who has given me the opportunity to lead and inspire others will be pleased that I had the freedom to choose, and chose wisely; the commitment to focus on what is important in life; the fidelity to overcome betrayal; the fortitude to face tough times; the forbearance to accept unwanted circumstances; the willingness to forgive others, lest I should not be forgiven; and the faith needed to trust that everyone I have met, and everything I have done, are all part of a bigger plan.

And the Author of that plan has taught me something else: Great leadership is not reserved for only the best, but rather for those who can honestly say they did their best.

Without faith a man can do nothing; with it all things are possible.
Sir William Osler
One of the Greatest Icons of Modern Medicine

978-0-595-48355-6
0-595-48355-0

Printed in the United States
115776LV00004B/244-273/P

9 780595 483556